THE ESSENTIALS OF EDUCATION

[XVIII]

FOUNDATIONS OF WALDORF EDUCATION

RUDOLF STEINER

The Essentials of Education

& Anthroposophic Press

*The publisher wishes to acknowledge the inspiration
and support of Connie and Robert Dulaney*

❖ ❖ ❖

These lectures are contained in the German *Die Methodik des Lehrens und die Lebensbedingungen des Erziehens* (vol. no. 308 in the Bibliographical Survey) published by Rudolf Steiner Verlag, Dornach, Switzerland. Translated from shorthand reports unrevised by the lecturer and first published in English in 1926 (translator unknown). Revised by Jesse Darrell in 1948 and further revised in 1968 by Rudolf Steiner Press, London. The lectures have been checked against the German text and revised by Anthroposophic Press for this edition.

Published by Anthroposophic Press
3390 Route 9, Hudson, NY 12534

Library of Congress Cataloging-in-Publication Data

Steiner, Rudolf, 1861–1925.
 [Methodik des Lehrens und die Lebensbedingnungen des Erziehens. English]
 The essentials of education / Rudolf Steiner.
  p. cm. — (Foundations of Waldorf Education ; 18)
 Includes bibliographical references (p.) and index.
 ISBN 0-88010-412-0
 1. Waldorf method of education. 2. Anthroposophy. I. Title. II. Series.
LB1029.W34S73513 1997
371.39—dc21   97-32011
                                                 CIP

10 9 8 7 6 5 4 3 2 1

Printed in the United States of America

Contents

Necessity for knowledge of the whole human being for a genuine education. The relationship between teacher and child is far-reaching. Before seven, the child is a "sense organ," and the body, soul, and spirit exist as a unity. The effects of the teacher's temperament on the child. The teacher's task during the three stages of childhood.

The demand for proof and the appropriate proof in spiritual matters. The descent of spirit into the body during the first seven years. The small child's natural religious devotion and the corresponding religious element needed in the teacher. After seven the child needs the teacher to be an artist. Humanity's development of materialism. The importance of imagery in teaching. Learning letters. Extremes in education.

Ancient humankind could "read" nature and human nature intuitively; modern science can "spell" but not "read." Learning to "read" children. Digestion before and after the change of teeth. Relationship between breath and heartbeat from seven to fourteen and how music harmonizes them. The etheric body and sculpting. The astral body and music. The I-being and speech. Eurythmy, music, and speech.

Introduction

The lectures that Rudolf Steiner gave in April, 1924, now freshly revised and republished as *The Essentials of Education* and *The Roots of Education*, represent a remarkable synthesis of Waldorf education as a practical manifestation of anthroposophy. This can be experienced through the flowing content of the lectures themselves and their place in the context of Steiner's work.

First in Stuttgart and then in Bern, Steiner delivered these lectures just eleven months before his death in March, 1925 and five years after the founding of the first Waldorf school in 1919. He had trained the teachers of the first Waldorf school and had the opportunity to have regular conversations with them in faculty meetings over several years.[1] Out of the practical experiences of working with the first schools, Steiner was in a position in April, 1924 to share the distilled essence, the most urgent themes arising from his educational work.

From a larger anthroposophic perspective, the contextual approach is also helpful. Some months before giving the lectures contained in this volume, Steiner spoke in England on the theme of karmic relationships.[2] In fact, *Essentials of Education* is embedded in his concurrent work on karmic relationships in

1. *Faculty Meetings with Rudolf Steiner 1919–1924*, 2 vols., Anthroposophic Press, Hudson, NY, forthcoming 1998 (GA 300a, b, c).
2. August, 1923, *Karmic Relationships: Esoteric Studies*, vol. 8, Rudolf Steiner Press, London, 1975.

that the educational lectures were given from April 8–11, "book-ended" by a karmic lecture on the sixth and twelfth of April in Dornach, Switzerland. Themes, such as human relationships, biography and temperaments, the influences of Sun and Moon, the need to see beyond the sense-perceptible, and much more, were developed in great detail in the karmic lectures, and they are echoed in the lectures on education in Stuttgart and Bern. Waldorf education works with the mysteries of time. Whether looking at life between death and rebirth or simply asking teachers to consider the effects of temperament on a child's later life, Steiner urges us to consider our present actions in terms of both the "before" and "after." More than any other form of education I am aware of, Waldorf education works with the flow of time.

I emphasize this point here, because the contextual picture shows how important it is that Waldorf education not be thought of as just a "method" of teaching or a way of getting through the challenges of the present, but that it be seen as a transformative, social impulse with far-reaching implications. "Contemporary humanity needs a complete renewal and strengthening of all spiritual life" (page 68).

In recommending the lectures in this book to parents, teachers, and friends of educational reform, I would like to call attention to several key themes that are especially worthy of consideration.

Knowledge of Human Nature and Relationships

Again and again, Rudolf Steiner returns to this central theme in these lectures—know the human being as expressed in body, soul, and spirit, and the teacher and parent will awaken in reverence and respect for their tasks. For example, Steiner speaks of child development and seven-year periods of growth; how the teacher's temperament affects the child's later development;

the fourfold human being; and specific subjects taught in relation to human conditions. His words, however, often apply to adults as well, as shown here:

> But we all carry an unconscious knowledge of the other within ourselves as unconscious perceptions, feelings, and, most importantly, impulses that lead to action.... Impressions [of another person] are pushed back down again, where they become a part of our soul's attitude toward the other person; we guide our behavior toward that person in terms of these first impressions. Then, too, what we call *empathy*—which is essentially one of the most significant impulses of human morality—also belongs to such unconscious knowledge of the human being. (page 4)

Considering some of the challenges parents and teachers face in working toward community, these inspiring thoughts are worthy of mutual study and conversation.

Education and Health

At a time when vast sums of money are spent each year in the health care industry, Steiner's indications in regard to teaching are more relevant today than ever before. In these lectures, he describes how the inner experiences of the teacher, whether perception, feeling, or thought—resonate within the soul of the child, which in turn "continues in the blood circulation and digestion, becoming a part of the foundation of health in later years" (page 28). There are many specific observations; for example, if teaching is too intellectual between the ages of seven and fourteen, the process of breathing out becomes congested. Thus, Waldorf teaching requires self-observation and ongoing self-training.

The New Curriculum

Some who are new to Waldorf education have observed that the curriculum appears to be defined—even rigid—compared to some other contemporary trends in public education. I respond to this in various ways, depending on the person, and I often point to child development and how curriculum "responds" to the changing consciousness of the child. For those who want a quick overview of the seven-year periods, there are some marvelous statements in *Essentials of Education*. Nevertheless, the issue of rigidity in the curriculum is real, in that any real content can become a "definition" rather than a way of knowing. Waldorf teachers are encouraged to avoid definitions in general, and instead work out of flexible artistry, educating feelings that are capable of metamorphosis. What is taught in an early grade may not awaken in full consciousness until high school or even later in life. When one works with the principle of metamorphosis, it is possible for the student to experience layers of meaning over time. The Waldorf curriculum is not a "thing" or "data base," but rather an indication of how a teacher can "read the developing being like a book that tells us what needs to be done in the teaching. The curriculum must reproduce what we read in the evolutionary process of the human being" (page 34). As with reading, child-based teaching is a *creative encounter*, one that can arise when the teacher is fully attentive. A true Waldorf curriculum is thus a *new* curriculum, one that must be created out of *direct perceptions of the developing child*. I like to say to my students at Antioch Graduate School that Waldorf teaching is a *life teacher training*.

All this has implications for teacher training, and Steiner refers to teacher preparation many times in both the Stuttgart and Bern (*Roots of Education*) lectures. If we take seriously the indications just mentioned, those who are preparing to teach in

Waldorf schools cannot be asked to simply ingest large quantities of information, whether Waldorf curriculum or anthroposophy in general. If they were to do that, after graduation they might dutifully "pour" their store of knowledge into the children or, failing that, revert to their pre-training concepts of teaching. The absorption of content without enough time to process it is like the wolf with too many stones in its belly.

Teachers in training need to learn new skills of active observation of children through long internship and *practice of the artistry of teaching*. This applies even in regard to the art classes given in teacher training; it is one thing to paint with adults in the peaceful environment of an adult education class and quite another to develop Old Testament stories with an active group of third graders. This requires many weeks of practice and guided reflection before being given the responsibility of class teaching.

When we read, for example, in *Essentials of Education* that writing should be taught out of drawing and how the *f* can evolve from a drawing of a fish, such statements are intended as examples, not as the "lesson plan" to be followed in rote fashion, with every *f* always swimming out of a fish. A teacher in training needs to learn the process, not the recipe; Steiner's indication was meant to stimulate the teacher's own creativity.

This is not achieved by reading these lines or by just taking courses. There was a time in history when human beings had instinctive intuitions about such matters, and the guide, or leader, was there to awaken and reinforce them. This is no longer sufficient for our modern times. What was formerly intuitive must now be conscious and free—deliberate probing for understanding the enigma of human nature.

This development in modern culture should pass through teacher training education like a magic breath and become a habit of the soul in the teachers…. The primary focus of a teacher's training should be the very heart of human nature itself. (pages 39–40.)

Once this habit of soul has been developed consciously, a new kind of intuition, or capacity for sensitivity, arises that allows for spontaneous responses to the needs of children. Rather than following rules of pedagogy, the prepared teacher is inwardly in tune with the class. Anthroposophy is an opportunity to practice this inner attunement.

The Arts

Chapter three contains a marvelous section on the arts in relation to the fourfold human being. In just a few pages, Rudolf Steiner characterizes what he had developed in earlier cycles in greater detail. In *Essentials of Education* he describes ways to observe the physical body of the child in breathing and movement, and then he portrays the *etheric* in relation to sculpting, the *astral* to music, and *I-experience* to human expression in speech. The new art of eurythmy resounds in the culmination of all four—the breath of movement, sculpting formation, and music and the spoken word.

It has been a deep concern to me in recent years that so many Waldorf schools do not have a fully developed eurythmy program, and that so few people choose to take up the practice of pedagogical eurythmy. We need to advocate for the modern art form that so strongly unites all aspects of the human being. Our atomistic, materialistic age needs the unity of human expression more than ever before. Waldorf education will not survive without this renewal.

Authority and Freedom

Contemporary educators and philosophers, such as Dewey, Kohl, Illich, Freire, Montessori, and others have discussed the role of the teacher and the free expression of the children in school. In the last lectures of *Essentials of Education*, we find the radical notion that children from ages seven to fourteen need to be in the presence of *natural authority*, "… children see what lives in the teacher's gestures, and they hear something revealed in how the teacher's words are spoken" (page 70). Children grow and learn *in relation* to what surrounds them. Even in our age of technology, human beings matter.

> This relationship to the teacher—the activity of the hidden forces between the child's heart and that of the teacher—is the most important aspect of the teaching method; the conditions for life in education are contained in this. (page 71)

If the child in the middle years is able to experience knowing through pictures and imagery, then an inner aesthetic sense is developed that forms a foundation for puberty and the unfolding intellect. "Proceeding to intellectual activity involves the human being looking into the self … after puberty the person truly experiences inner freedom" (page 66). What was learned through the revered authority during the younger years can create soul conditions that foster a full experience of the I-being later on—a way of being that allows "human beings to act as if God were acting in them" (page 75).

These and other insights found in this volume can help us all become advocates for something new in education today. If readers can devote some time to carefully working through these lectures, there is a possibility that we can change the paradigm and change the context of the contemporary debate on education. Rather than continually accepting the framework given by the media on what constitutes good schools, those who work with an anthroposophically inspired form of education can reframe the discussion to focus on questions of human nature and relationship, education for health, the new curriculum, teacher training, the arts, and a new approach to understanding authority and freedom.

In regard to the essentials of education, let us no longer remain silent.

TORIN M. FINSER, Ph.D.
Director, Waldorf Teacher Training
Antioch Graduate School, Keene, New Hampshire

Lecture One

Dear friends! Our assignment for this educational conference is to answer the question: What is the role of education and teaching to be for the future in terms of both the individual and society? Anyone who looks with an unbiased eye at modern civilization and its various institutions can hardly question the importance of this theme today (by "today" I mean the current decade in history). This theme touches on questions deep in the souls and hearts of a great many people.

Knowledge of the Whole Human Being

In our modern civilization, we have seen people develop a peculiar attitude toward their own being. For over a century, our civilization has witnessed the ambitious development of natural science and its consequences for humanity; indeed, all of contemporary life has been affected by the knowledge and ideas engendered by natural science. From the perspective of natural science, however, wherever we look and no matter how exactly we observe the mineral kingdom and develop ideas of nature's other realms, one thing is clear: although there was close and intimate self-knowledge of human beings in earlier cultural epochs, this is no longer the situation today. Whatever achievements natural science may have brought to humankind, it cannot be applied directly to the human being.

We can ask: What are the laws that govern the development of the world beyond humankind? However, none of the answers come close to the essence of what lives within the limits of the human skin. Answers are so inadequate that people today haven't a clue about the ways that external natural processes are actually transformed within the human being through breathing, blood circulation, nutrition, and so on.

Consequently, we have come to the point where, even in terms of the soul, we do not look at the soul itself, but study its external manifestations in the human body. Today people experiment on human beings. However, I don't intend to criticize psychological or pedagogical experimentation. We must acknowledge what can be accomplished in this way, but mostly this approach is a symptom of our cultural milieu, since in fact the results of such experiments tell us little about the human being.

In earlier times, people had a sense of inner empathy with the spirit and soul of other human beings, which gave them an intuitive impression of the soul's inner experiences; it made sense that what one knew about the inner spirit and soul life would explain external physical manifestations. Now, we do just the opposite. People experiment with external aspects and processes very effectively, since all contemporary natural science is effective. The only thing that has been demonstrated, however, is that, given our modern views of life, we take seriously only what is sense-perceptible and what the intellect can comprehend with the help of the senses. Consequently, we have come to a point where we no longer have the capacity to really observe the inner human being; we are often content to observe its outer shell. We are further removed from the human being. Indeed, the very methods that have so eagerly illuminated life in the outer world—the working of nature— have robbed us of the most basic access between souls.

Our wonderfully productive civilization has brought us very close to certain natural phenomena, but it has also driven us away from the human being. It should be obvious that the aspect of our culture most harmed by this situation is education—everything related to human development and teaching children. Once we can understand those we are to shape, we will be able to educate and teach, just as painters must understand the nature and quality of colors before they can paint, and sculptors must first understand their materials before they can create, and so on. If this is true of the arts that deal with physical materials, isn't it all the more true of an art that works with the noblest of all materials, the material that only the human being can work with—human life, the human being and human development?

These issues remind us that all education and all teaching must spring from the fountain of real knowledge of the human being. In the Waldorf schools, we are attempting to create such an art of education, solidly based on true understanding of the human being, and this educational conference is about the educational methods of Waldorf education.

Knowledge of the human being! I can hear people saying how far we have come in our knowledge of the human being in our time! I must reply that, although we have made extraordinary advances in our knowledge of the human physical body, the human being is really body, soul, and spirit. The worldview at the foundation of Waldorf education—that is, anthroposophic spiritual science—consists equally of knowledge of the human body, the human soul, and the human spirit, being careful to avoid any imbalance.

In the following lectures, I will have much more to say about such knowledge of the human being. But first, let me point out that true knowledge of the human being does not come from merely looking at an isolated individual with three aspects. Knowledge of the human being primarily tries to keep sight of what happens among human beings during earthly life.

When one human being encounters another, a fully conscious knowledge of each other's being does not develop between them—such a thing would be absurd. We couldn't begin to interact socially if we were to view one another with analytical questions in mind. But we all carry an unconscious knowledge of the other within ourselves as unconscious perceptions, feelings, and, most importantly, impulses that lead to action. We will see that knowledge of the human being has suffered a great deal in the modern world, and this has given rise to many social evils. In a sense, however, knowledge of human beings has only withdrawn to deeper levels of the unconscious than ever before. Nevertheless, it is still available to us, since, if it weren't, we would pass each other with no means of understanding one another.

It is certainly true that when one person meets another—whether or not we are aware of it—sympathies and antipathies arise, and impressions are formed. They tell us whether the other person can be allowed to get close, or if we would prefer to stay clear of that other person. Other impressions arise as well. Immediately, we may say, "This is an intelligent person," or "that person is not very gifted." I could mention hundreds and hundreds of impressions that spring from the depths of the soul. During most of our life, such impressions are pushed back down again, where they become a part of our soul's attitude toward the other person; we guide our behavior toward that person in terms of these first impressions. Then, too, what we call *empathy*—which is essentially one of the most significant impulses of human morality—also belongs to such unconscious knowledge of the human being.

The Relationship between Teacher and Child

In our adult interactions, we use our knowledge of the human being so unconsciously that we are unaware of it, but we nevertheless act according to it. In our capacity as teachers, however, the relationship between our human soul as teacher and the child's human soul must be much more conscious so that we have a formative effect on the child. But we also must become aware of our own teacher's soul so that we experience what is necessary to establish the right mood, the right teaching artistry, and the right empathy with the child's soul. All of these things are necessary to adequately performing our educational and teaching task. We are immediately reminded that the most important aspect in education and teaching is what occurs between the teacher's soul and the child's soul.

Let's start with this knowledge of the human being; it is knowledge with "soft edges." It lacks sharp contours to the extent that it is not pointed directly at any one person. Rather, over the course of the educational relationship it glides, as it were, weaving here and there between what happens in the teacher's soul and in the child's soul. In certain ways, it is difficult to be very sure of what is happening, since it is all very subtle. When we teach, something is present that flows like a stream, constantly changing. It is necessary to develop a vision that allows us to seize anything that is developing between human beings in this intimate way.

We might consider a few specific examples as an introduction to the way these currents form. In doing this, we must consider one thing: when we deal with a human being "in-process," a growing child, knowledge of the human being is too often applied in an exact way. We take the child at a specific point in life and get to work, asking about the child's developmental forces, how they operate at that particular age, and so on, and we ask how we can properly meet these developmental forces at this particular time. But knowledge of the human being as intended here is not concerned only with these moments of experience, but with the person's whole earthly life. It is not really as easy as observing a precise time span in a human life. But educators and teachers must be able to look at the whole human life; whatever we do in the eighth or ninth year will have effects upon the forty- or fifty-year-old adult, as we will see a little later.

As a teacher, anything I do to a child during the years of education will sink deeply into the physical, psychological, and spiritual nature of that individual. Whatever I do that plants a seed at the beginning of life will in some way go on living and working for decades beneath the surface, reappearing in remarkable ways many years later, perhaps not until the very end of life. It is possible to affect childhood in the right way if we consider not just childhood but all of human life as seen from the perspective of a real knowledge of the human being.

This is the knowledge I have in mind as I give you a few examples about the intimate ways the teacher's soul can affect the child's soul. I will present only a few indications for today—we will go into greater detail later. We can understand how to prepare the intellect for activities of the will only if we can answer this question: What happens between the teacher and the child, simply because the teacher and the child are present together, each with a unique nature and temperament—a particular character, level of development, constitution of body and soul? Before we even begin to teach and educate, the teacher and the child are both present. There is already an interaction. The teacher's relationship to the child presents the first important question.

Rather than wandering off in abstractions, let's just look at specifics; we shall examine one particular characteristic in human nature—the temperament. Let's not view a child's temperament, which of course offers us no choice—we must educate each human being regardless of temperament (we will speak later of the children's temperaments); but let's begin rather by looking at the *teacher's* temperament. The teacher approaches the child with a very specific temperament—choleric, sanguine, melancholic, or phlegmatic. The question is: As educators, what can we do to control our own temperaments; how can we perhaps educate ourselves in relation to our own temperament? To answer this question we must first look directly at the fundamental question: How does a teacher's temperament affect the child, just by being what it is?

The Choleric Temperament

We will begin with the *choleric* temperament. The teacher's choleric temperament may be expressed when the teacher lets loose and vents anger. We will see later how teachers can control themselves. Let's assume for starters that the teacher has a temper, which is expressed in powerful, vehement expressions. It may drive the teacher to act or handle the child in ways that arise from a choleric temperament, which is regretted later on. The teacher may do things in the presence of the child that cause fright (we will see the fragile nature of a child's soul). The child's fright may not last for long, but nevertheless take root deep in the child's physical organism. A choleric adult may have such an effect that the child always approaches the teacher in fear, whereas another child may just feel pressured. In other words, there is a very specific way the choleric temperament works on a child, having subtle, intimate effects.

Let's consider the preschool child. At that stage a child is a single entity; the child's three members—body, soul, and spirit—separate later on. Between birth and the change of teeth (which is a very important point in the child's development) there is a period of time when the child is, for all practical purposes, entirely a sensory organ; this is not generally emphasized enough.

Let's imagine a sensory organ—the eye, for example. This eye is organized in very integral ways that unite with the impressions made by colors. Without a person having any say in the matter, the slightest external impression is immediately transformed into activity, which is only then experienced in the soul. The entire life of the child before the change of teeth is ruled in this way by sensory perceptions that impress the soul. All inner experiences are a kind of soul experience.

Children absorb impressions from all the people around them with the same intensity that sensory organs receive impressions from the environment. The way we move around children—whether slowly, displaying a relaxed soul and spirit or with stormily, showing a heavy soul and spirit—is absorbed by them; they are completely sensory. We might say that an adult tastes with the mouth, or with the palate or tongue. Children, however, experience taste in the very depths of their organism; it's as though the sense of taste were spread throughout the whole body. This is also true of the other senses. The effects of light relate internally to a child's respiratory system and circulation. What is to an adult a separate visual perception, the child experiences in the whole body; and without any forethought, a child's will impulses take the shape of reflexes. A child's whole body responds reflexively to every impression in the environment.

This means that the spirit, soul, and body of a small child are still undifferentiated, still interwoven as a unified whole. The soul and spirit work in the body and directly influence the circulatory and digestive processes. It is remarkable how close a child's soul and metabolism are to each other and how closely they work together. Only later, at the change of teeth, does the soul element become differentiated from the metabolism. Every stimulation of a child's soul is transcribed in the blood circulation, breathing, and digestion. This means that a child's environment affects a child's whole body.

And so, when a choleric teacher gets near a child and lets loose with fits of temper, anything done under this influence— if the teacher has not learned to deal with this—enters the child's soul and takes root in the body. The remarkable thing is that it sinks into the foundations of the child's being, and anything implanted in the growing human body reappears later. Just as a seed is planted in the autumn and reappears in the spring as a plant, so whatever is planted as a seed in a child of eight or nine comes out again in the adult of forty-five or fifty. And we can see the effects of an uncontrolled choleric teacher's temperament in the form of metabolic illnesses in the adult, or even in the very old.

If we could only verify the reason this or that person suffers from arthritis, or why another has all kinds of metabolic disorders, poor digestion, or gout, there would be only one answer: many of these things can be attributed to the violent temperament of a teacher who dealt with the child at an early age.

If we achieve pedagogical understanding by looking at the whole human being and not just at the child—which is much more comfortable—it becomes clear that education and teaching play a central role in the course of human life. We see how often happiness or unhappiness in the spirit, soul, or physical life is related to a person's education and schooling. Just consider this: doctors are asked by older people to correct the mistakes of their educators, when in fact the problems have sunk so deeply into the person that no more can be done. The impressions on the child's soul have been transformed into physical effects, and the psychological interacts with the physical; knowing all this, we begin to pay attention in the right way, and we acquire a proper appreciation for teaching methods and what is required for a viable education according to the reality of human nature.

The Phlegmatic Temperament

Now, let us consider the phlegmatic teacher. We will assume again that this teacher makes no attempt at self-knowledge or self-education regarding temperament. It can be said of the phlegmatic that whatever comes to the child from such a person is not strong enough to meet the inner activity of the child's soul. The inner impulses want to come out, to flow out, and the child wants to be active, but the teacher is phlegmatic and just lets things be. This teacher is unable to engage what flows out of the child, failing to encounter it with enough impressions and influences. It's as if one were trying to breathe in a rarefied atmosphere, to use a physical analogy. The child's soul "asphyxiates" when the teacher is phlegmatic. When we see such a child in later life, we can understand why some people are nervous or suffer from neurasthenia, and so on. By going back to their childhood, we find that it is related to the uncontrolled phlegmatic temperament of an educator who failed to do important things with the child.

We might even be able to explain widespread cultural pathologies in this way. Why is it that nervous diseases such as depression are so widespread today? You might be thinking I'm trying to convince you that, when the current generation of neurasthenic adults was being educated, the whole teaching profession was phlegmatic! I will reply that it did consist of phlegmatics—not in the usual sense of the word, but in a much deeper sense. We are speaking of the historical period of the nineteenth century when materialism rose. The materialistic worldview turns away from the human being, and develops a monstrous indifference in the teacher toward the most intimate movements of the souls of those being educated.

If, in an unbiased way, we can observe the cultural manifestations of the modern era, we find that a person may be a phlegmatic in that sense, even though that same person might angrily react to a child who spilled ink yelling: "You should not do that! You should not throw ink because you are angry; I'll throw it back at you, you rascal!" Such outbursts of choleric temper were not the exception during the time I just described, nor am I suggesting that there was any shortage of sanguine or melancholic teachers. But in their actual teaching, they were still phlegmatics and acted phlegmatic. The materialistic worldview was uninterested in meeting the human being, and certainly not the growing human being. Phlegma became an aspect of all education in the materialistic era. And it has a lot to do with the appearance of nervous disease, or nervous disorganization, in our culture. We will look at this in detail later. Nevertheless, we see the effect of phlegmatic teachers whose very presence next to children triggers nervous disorders.

The Melancholic Temperament

If a teacher succumbs to a melancholic temperament and becomes too self-absorbed, the thread of the child's spirit and soul nature is constantly in danger of breaking, dampening the feeling life. In this way, the melancholic teacher's influence causes the child to suppress soul impulses. Instead of expressing them, the child retreats within.

If a teacher gives in to a melancholic temperament while with children, it can lead in later life to breathing and circulatory problems. Teachers should not educate with only childhood in mind. And doctors should look beyond the specific onset of disease to a particular age, with a capacity to observe human life as one connected whole. In this way, people can see that many cases of heart trouble between forty and forty-five began with the whole mood generated by the uncontrolled melancholic temperament of a teacher.

Obviously, when we observe the spiritual and psychic imponderables that play between the teacher's soul and that of the child, we must ask: How should teachers and education professionals educate themselves about the various temperaments? We can understand that it is not enough for the teacher to say, "I was born with my temperament; I can't help myself." First of all, this is untrue, and even if it were true, the human race would have died out long ago due to wrong education.

The Sanguine Temperament

The teacher who gives full vent to a sanguine temperament is susceptible to all kinds of impressions. When a student makes a mess, the teacher looks the other way instead of getting angry. A student may whisper to a neighbor, and the teacher again looks the other way. This is typical of the sanguine temperament; impressions come quickly, but do not penetrate deeply. Such a teacher may call on a little girl to ask a brief question; but the teacher is not interested in her for long and almost immediately sends her back to her seat. This teacher is completely sanguine.

Again, if we look at the whole human life, we can trace many cases of insufficient vitality and zest for life—which may even be pathological—to the effects of a teacher's undisciplined sanguine temperament. Without self-knowledge, a teacher's sanguine temperament suppresses vitality, dampens the zest for life, and weakens the will that wells up from the child's essential being.

These relationships, as revealed by a spiritual science, help us understand the human being. With this in mind, we can realize how comprehensive the real art of education is; we can see the way teaching must view the nature of the human being and the limits of looking only at what is immediately present and obvious. This is not enough, and we are faced with the essential demand of our current civilization—the civilization that has already brought enough discord to human existence.

But, given the various simple and superficial observations of research, statistics, and other ingenious methods—which form the basis of almost all education and didacticism—how can we educate in a way that equally considers the whole human experience and the eternal nature of the human being that shines through human experience? Something much deeper appears in relation to these matters. As an introduction, I have tried to show you what is at play between teacher and student just because they are there—even before anything is done consciously, but merely because the two are there. This is especially revealed in the different temperaments.

It will be argued that there comes a point where we must begin to educate. Yes, and immediately we encounter the opinion that anyone can teach someone else whatever one has already learned. If I have learned something, I am, so to speak, qualified to teach it to someone else. People frequently fail to notice that there is an inner attitude of temperament, character, and so on, behind everything a teacher brings to teaching, regardless of self-education, formal training, or assimilated knowledge. Here, too, a real knowledge of the human being leads more deeply into human nature itself.

Let's inquire, then, about teaching an unschooled child something we have learned. Is it enough to present it to the child just as we learned it? It certainly is not. Now I will speak of an observed phenomenon, the results of a real observation of the whole life of a human being in body, soul, and spirit. It concerns the first period of life, from birth until the change of teeth.

The Teacher and the Three Stages of Childhood

When we understand the interrelationship between teacher and child in terms of the temperaments, we see that, during this first stage of life, what we have learned is relatively unimportant to teaching and educating a child. The most important considerations have to do with the kind of person one is, what impressions the child receives, and whether or not one is worthy of imitation.

As far as this life period is concerned, if a civilization never spoke of education and in its elementary, primitive way simply educated, it would have a much healthier outlook than ours. This was true of the ancient Eastern regions, which had no education in our sense of the word. There the adult's body, soul, and spirit was allowed to affect the child so that the child could take this adult as a guide, moving a muscle when the teacher moved a muscle and blinking when the teacher blinked. The teacher was trained to do this in a way that enabled the child to imitate. Such a teacher was not as the Western "pedagogue," but the Eastern *data*.[1] A certain instinctive quality was behind this. Even today, it is obvious that what I have learned is totally irrelevant in terms of my ability to effectively teach a child before the change of teeth. After the change of teeth, the teacher's knowledge begins to have some significance; but this is again lost, if I merely impart what I learned as it lives in me. It must all be transformed artistically and made into images, as we shall see later. I must awaken invisible forces between the child and myself.

In the second life period, between the change of teeth and puberty, it is much more important that I transform my knowledge into visual imagery and living forms, unfolding it and allowing it to flow into the child. What a person has learned is important only for children after puberty until the early twenties.

For the small child before the change of teeth, the most important thing in education is the teacher's own being. The most important element for teaching the child between the

---

1. In Sanskrit, "the giver."

change of teeth and puberty is the teacher who can enter living artistry. Only after the age of fourteen or fifteen can the child really claim what the teacher has learned. This continues until after the early twenties, when the child is fully grown (even though it's true that we call the teenager a young lady or young gentleman). At twenty years, the young person can meet another human being on equal terms, even when the other is older.

Things like this enable us to look deep into the human nature—and we shall see how this is deepened in the presence of true human wisdom. We come to realize what has often been thought—that we do not become acquainted with the teacher by examining what the person knows after going through college. That would show us only a capacity for lecturing on some subject, perhaps something suitable for students between fourteen and twenty. As far as earlier stages are concerned, what the teacher does in this sense has no relevance whatever. The qualities necessary for these early periods must be assessed on a very different basis.

Thus, we see that a fundamental issue in teaching and education is the question of who the teacher is. What must really live in the children, what must vibrate and well up into their very hearts, wills, and eventually into their intellect, lives initially in the teachers. It arises simply through who they are, through their unique nature, character, and soul attitude, and through what they bring the children out of their own self-development. So we can see how a true knowledge of the human being, cultivated into embracing everything, can be the single foundation for a true art of teaching and fulfill the living needs of education.

In the lectures that follow, I want to go into these two things more fully—the pedagogy, and the living needs of education.

Lecture Two

Yesterday I spoke of the teacher's encounter with the children. Today I will try to describe the child, as a growing being, and the experience of encountering the teacher. A more exact observation of the forces active in the development of the human being shows that at the beginning of a child's earthly life we must distinguish three distinct stages of life. After we have gained a knowledge of the human being and the ability to perceive the characteristics of these three stages, we can begin to educate in a way that is true to the facts—or rather, an education that is true to the human being.

The Nature of Proof in Spiritual Matters

The first stage of life ends with the change of teeth. Now I know that there is a certain amount of awareness these days concerning the changes that occur in the body and soul of children at this stage of life. Nevertheless, it is not sufficient to enable perception of all that happens in the human being at this tender age; we must come to understand this in order to become educators. The appearance of teeth—not the inherited, baby teeth—is merely the most obvious sign of a complete transformation of the whole human being. Much more is happening within the organism, though not as perceptible outwardly; its most radical expression is the appearance of the second teeth.

If we consider this we can see that contemporary physiology and psychology simply cannot penetrate the human being with any real depth, since their particular methods (excellent though they may be) were developed to observe only outer physical nature and the soul as it manifests in the body. As I said yesterday, the task of anthroposophic spiritual science is to penetrate in every way the whole human development of body, soul, and spirit.

First, however, we must eliminate a certain assumption. This preconception is inevitably a stumbling block to anyone who approaches the Waldorf education movement without a basic study of anthroposophy. I do not mean for a moment that we simply ignore objections to this kind of education. On the contrary. Those who have a spiritual foundation such as anthroposophy cannot be the least bit fanatical; they will always fully consider any objections to their viewpoints. Consequently, they fully understand the frequent argument against anthroposophic education. But, these things still must be proven.

Now, people have a lot to say about proofs with no clear idea of what that means. I cannot present a detailed lecture on the methods of proof in the various spheres of life and knowledge; but I would like to be clear about a certain comparison.

What do people mean when they say that something requires "proof"? The whole trend of human evolution since the fourteenth century has been to validate judgments through visual observation—that is to say, through sense perception. It was a very different matter before the current era, or before the fourteenth century. But we fail to realize today that our ancestors had a very different view of the world. In a certain sense we feel proud when we consider the development that has occurred in recent centuries. We look condescendingly at what people did during the Middle Ages, for example, considering them childish and primitive. But it is an age about which we really know nothing and call the "Dark Ages." Try to imagine how our successors will speak of us—if they are as arrogant in their thinking as we are! If they turn out to be so conceited, we will seem just as childish to them as medieval people appear to us.

During the ages before the fourteenth century, humans perceived the world of the senses, and also comprehended with the intellect. The intelligence of the medieval monastic schools is too often underestimated. The inner intelligence and conceptual faculty was much more highly developed than the modern and chaotic conceptual faculty, which is really driven by, and limited to, natural phenomena; anyone who is objective and impartial can observe this. In those days, anything that the intellect and senses perceived in the universe required validation from the divine, spiritual realm. The fact that sense revelation had to be sanctioned by divine revelation was not merely an abstract principle; it was a common, very human feeling and observation. A manifestation in the world of the senses could be considered valid only when knowledge of it could be proven and demonstrated in terms of the divine, spiritual world.

This situation changed, gradually at first, one mode of knowledge replacing the other. Today, however, it has come to the point where we only acknowledge the validity of something—even in the spiritual world—when it can be proven through the senses. Something is validated when statements about spiritual life can be confirmed by experiment and observation. Why does everyone ask for a demonstration of matters that are really related to spirit? People ask you to make an experiment or sense observation that provides proof.

This is what people want, because they have lost faith in the reality of the human being's inner activity; they have lost faith in the possibility that intuitions can emerge from the human being when looking at ordinary life, at sensory appearances and the intellect. Humanity has really weakened inwardly, and is no longer conscious of the firm foundation of an inner, creative life. This has had a deep influence on all areas of practical life, and most of all on education.

Proofs, such as external sensory appearances, through observation and experiment, may be compared to a man who notices that an unsupported object falls, and that it is attracted by the Earth's gravity and therefore must be supported until it rests on solid ground. And then this man says, "Go ahead, tell me that the Earth and the other heavenly bodies hover freely in space, but I cannot understand it. Everything must be supported or it will fall." Nevertheless, the Earth, Sun, and other heavenly bodies do not fall. We must completely change our way of thinking, when we move from earthly conditions into the cosmos. In cosmic space, heavenly bodies support one another; the laws of Earth do not apply there.

This is also true of spiritual facts. When we speak of the material nature of plants, animals, minerals, or human beings, we must prove our statements through experiment and sense observation. This kind of proof, like the example mentioned, suggests that an object must be supported. In the free realm of the spirit, however, truths support one another. The only validation required is their mutual support. Thus, in representing spiritual reality, every idea must be placed clearly within the whole, just as Earth or any other heavenly body moves freely in cosmic space. Truths must support one another. Anyone who tries to understand the spiritual realm must first examine truths coming from other directions, and how they support the one truth through the free activity of their "gravitational force" of proof, as it were. In this way, that single truth is kept free in the cosmos, just as a heavenly body is supported freely in the cosmos by the countering forces of gravity. A capacity to conceive of the spiritual in this way must become an essential inner quality of human beings; otherwise, though we may be able to understand and educate the soul aspect, we will be unable to understand and educate the spirit that also lives and moves in the human being.

The Individual's Entry into the World

When human beings enter the physical world of sensation, their physical body is provided by the parents and ancestors. Even natural science knows this, although such discoveries will become complete only in the remote future. Spiritual science teaches that this is only one aspect of the human being; the other part unites with what arises from the father and mother; it descends as a spirit and soul being from the realm of spirit and soul.

Between the previous earthly life and the present one, this being passed through a long period of existence from the previous death to rebirth; it had experiences in the spiritual world between death and rebirth, just as on Earth, between birth and death, we have bodily experiences communicated through the senses, intellect, feelings, and will. The essence of these spiritual experiences descends, unites at first only loosely with the physical nature of the human being during the embryonic period, and hovers around the person, lightly and externally like an aura, during the first period of childhood between birth and the change of teeth. This being of spirit and soul who comes down from the spiritual world—a being just as real as the one who comes from the body of the mother—is more loosely connected with the physical body than it is later in human life. This is the why the child lives much more outside the body than an adult does.

This is only another way of expressing what I said in yesterday's lecture, namely, that during the first period of life the child is in the highest degree and by its whole nature a being of sense. The child is like a sense organ. The surrounding impressions ripple, echo and sound through the whole organism because the child is not so inwardly bound up with its body as is the case in later life, but lives in the environment with its freer spiritual and soul nature. Hence the child is receptive to all the impressions coming from the environment.

Now, what is the relation between the human being as a whole and what we receive from the father and mother strictly through heredity? If we study the development of the human being with vision that truly creates ideas instead of mere proofs as described—a vision that looks at the spiritual and the evolution of the human being—we find that everything in the organism depends on hereditary forces in exactly the same way as the first, so-called baby teeth do. We only need to perceive, with precise vision, the difference in the ways the second teeth and the first are formed. In this way, we have a tangible expression of the processes occurring in the human being between birth and the change of teeth.

During this stage the forces of heredity hold sway in the physical body, and the whole human being becomes a kind of model with which the spirit and soul element work, imitating the surrounding impressions. If we place ourselves in the soul of a child relative to the environment and realize how every spiritual impulse is absorbed into the whole being—how with every movement of the hand, every expression, every look in the eyes of another the child senses the spirit inherent in the adult and allows it to flow in—then we will also perceive how, during the first seven years, another being is building itself on the foundation of the model provided by heredity. As human beings, the earthly world actually gives us, through hereditary forces, a model on which to build the second human being, who is really born with the change of teeth. The first teeth in the body are eliminated by what wants to replace them; this new element, which belongs to the human being's individuality, advances and casts off heredity. This is true of the whole human organism. During the first seven years of life, the organism was a product of earthly forces and a kind of model. As such it is cast off, just as we get rid of the body's outgrowths by cutting our nails, hair, and so on. The human being is molded anew with the change of teeth just as our outer form is perpetually eliminated. In this case, however, the first being, or product of physical heredity, is completely replaced by a second, who develops under the influence of the forces that the human being brings from pre-earthly life. Thus, during the period between birth and the change of teeth, the human hereditary forces related to the physical evolutionary stream fight against the forces of a pre-earthly existence, which accompany the individuality of each human being from the previous earthly life.

The Religious Nature of Childhood

It is essential not to merely understand these things theoretically, which is the habitual way of thinking today. This is the kind of fact that must be understood by the whole inner human being from the perspective of the child, and only then from the standpoint of the educator. If we understand what is happening from the perspective of a child, we find that the soul-being of the child—with everything brought from pre-earthly life from the realm of soul and spirit—is entirely devoted to the physical activities of human beings in the surroundings. This relationship can be described only as a *religious* one. It is a religious relationship that descends into the sphere of nature and moves into the outer world. It is important, however, to understand what is meant by such term.

Ordinarily, one speaks of "religious" relationships today in the sense of a consciously developed adult religion. Relevant to this is the fact that, in religious life, the spirit and soul elements of the adult rise into the spiritual element in the universe and surrender to it. The religious relationship is a self-surrendering to the universe, a prayer for divine grace in the surrender of the self. In the adult, it is completely immersed in a spiritual element. The soul and spirit are yielded to the surroundings. To speak of the child's body being absorbed by the environment in terms of a religious experience thus seems like we are turning things around the wrong way. Nevertheless, it is a truly religious experience—transposed into the realm of nature. The child is surrendered to the environment and lives in the external world in reverent, prayerful devotion, just as the eye detaches itself from the rest of the organism and surrenders to the environment. It is a religious relationship transferred to the natural realm.

If we want a picture, or symbol, of the spirit and soul processes in the adult's religious experience, we should form a real idea in our souls of the child's body up to the change of teeth. The life of the child is "religious," but religious in a way that refers to the things of nature. It is not the *soul* of the child that is surrendered to the environment, but the blood circulation, breathing activities, and the nutritional process through the food taken in. All of these things are surrendered to the environment—the blood circulation, breathing, and digestive processes pray to the environment.

The Priestly Nature of Teaching

These expressions may seem contradictory, but their very contradiction represents the truth. We must observe such things with our whole being, not theoretically. If we observe the struggle unfolding in the child before us—within this fundamental, natural religious element—if we observe the struggle between the hereditary forces and what the individual's forces develop as the second human being through the power brought from pre-earthly life, then, as teachers, we also develop a religious mood. But, whereas the child with a physical body develops the religious mood of the believer, the teacher, in gazing at the wonders that occur between birth and the change of teeth, develops a "priestly" religious attitude. The position of teacher becomes a kind of priestly office, a ritual performed at the altar of universal human life—not with a sacrificial victim to be led to death, but with the offering of human nature itself, to be awakened to life. Our task is to ferry into earthly life the aspect of the child that came from the divine spiritual world. This, with the child's own forces, forms a second organism from the being that came to us from the divine spiritual life.

Pondering such things awakens something in us like a priestly attitude in education. Until this priestly feeling for the first years of childhood has become a part of education as a whole, education will not find the conditions that bring it to life. If we merely try to understand the requirements of education intellectually, or try to rationally design a method of education based on external observations of a child's nature, at best we accomplish a quarter education. A complete educational method cannot be formulated by the intellect alone, but must flow from the whole human nature—not merely from the part that observes externally in a rational way, but the whole that deeply and inwardly experiences the secrets of the universe.

Few things have a more wonderful effect on the human heart than seeing inner spirit and soul elements released day to day, week to week, month to month, year to year, during the first period of childhood. We see how, beginning with chaotic limb movements, the glance filled with rapture by the outer, the play of expressions that do not yet seem to belong to the child, something develops and impresses itself on the surface of the human form that arises from the center of the human being, where the divine spiritual being is unfolding in its descent from pre-earthly life. When we can make this divine office of education a concern of the heart, we understand these things in such a way that we say: "Here the Godhead Who has guided the human being until birth is revealed again in the impression of the human organism; the living Godhead is there to see; God is gazing into us." This, out of the teacher's own individuality, will lead, not to something learned by rote, but to a living method of education and instruction, a method that springs from the inner being.

This must be our attitude to the growing human being; it is essential to any educational method. Without this fundamental attitude, without this priestly element in the teacher (this is said, of course, in a cosmic sense), education cannot be continued. Therefore, any attempt to reform the methods of education must involve a return of the intellectual element, which has become dominant since the fourteenth century, to the domain of soul and feelings, to move toward what flows from human nature as a whole, not just from the head. If we look at the child without preconceptions, the child's own nature will teach us to read these things.

The Effects of a Teacher's Inner Development on the Child

Now, what has been the real course of civilization since the fourteenth century? As a result of the great transition, or cultural revolution, that has occurred since then, we can only perceive what is expressed, as it were, from internal to external existence. Grasping at externals has become a matter of course for modern human beings to the degree that we are no longer aware of any other possibility. We have arrived at a condition in historical evolution that is considered "right" in an absolute sense—not merely a condition that suits our time.

People can no longer feel or perceive in a way that was possible before the fourteenth century. In those days, people observed matters of the spirit in an imbalanced way, just as people now observe the things of nature. But the human race had to pass through a stage in which it could add the observation of purely natural elements to an earlier human devotion to the world of spirit and soul that excluded nature. This materializing process, or swing downward, was necessary; but we must realize that, in order that civilized humanity not be turned into a wasteland in our time, there must be a new turn, a turning toward spirit and soul. The awareness of this fact is the essence of all endeavors such as that of Waldorf school education, which is rooted in what a deeper observation of human evolution reveals as necessary for our time. We must find our way back to the spirit and soul; for this we must first clearly recognize how we removed ourselves from them in the first place. There are many today who have no such understanding and, therefore, view anything that attempts to lead us back to the spirit as, well, not really the point, shall we say.

We can find remarkable illustrations of this attitude. I would like to mention one, but only parenthetically. There is a chapter (incidentally, a very interesting chapter in some ways) in Maurice Maeterlinck's new book *The Great Riddle*.[1] Its subject is the anthroposophic way of viewing the world. He describes anthroposophy, and he also describes me (if you will forgive a personal reference). He has read many of my books and makes a very interesting comment. He says that, at the beginning of my books, I seem to have a levelheaded, logical, and shrewd mind. In the later chapters, however, it seems as if I had lost my

---

1. Maurice Maeterlinck (1862–1949), Belgian poet, dramatist, and essayist. In Paris he gained a reputation through Symbolist verse and became a leading Symbolist playwright. He was awarded a Nobel prize for literature in 1911.

senses. It may very well appear this way to Maeterlinck; subjectively he has every right to his opinion. Why shouldn't I seem levelheaded, logical and scientific to him in the first chapters, and insane in later ones?

Of course, Maeterlinck has a right to think this way, and nobody wants to stop him. The question is, however, whether such an attitude is not really absurd. Indeed, it does become absurd when you consider this: I have, unfortunately, written a great many books in my life (as you can see from the unusual appearance of the book table here). No sooner have I finished writing one, than I begin another. When Maurice Maeterlinck reads the new book, he will discover once again that, in the first chapters I am shrewd, levelheaded and scientific, and lose my senses later on. Then I begin to write a third book; the first chapters again are reasonable and so forth. Consequently, if nothing else, I seem to have mastered the art of becoming at will a completely reasonable human being in the early part of a book and—equally by choice—a lunatic later, only to return to reason when I write the next book. In this way, I take turns being reasonable and a lunatic. Naturally, Maeterlinck has every right to find this; but he misses the absurdity of such an idea. A modern man of his importance thus falls into absurdities; but this, as I say, is only an interpolation.

Many people are completely unaware that their judgments do not spring from the source of human nature but from elements implanted in our outer culture since the fourteenth century as a result of the materialistic system of life and education. The duty of teachers, of educators—really the duty of all human beings that have anything to do with children—is to look more deeply into the human being. In other words, we need to become more aware of how anything acting as a stimulus in the environment continues to vibrate in the child. We must be very clear that, in this sense, we are dealing with imponderables.

Children are aware, whenever we do something in their environment, of the thoughts behind a hand-gesture or facial expression. Children intuit them: they do not, obviously, interpret facial features, since what operates instead is a much more powerful inner connection between the child and adult than will exist later between adults. Consequently, we must never allow ourselves to feel or think anything around children that should not be allowed to ripple on within the child. The rule of thumb for all relationships in early education must be this: Whether in perception, feeling, or thought, whatever we do around children must be done in such a way that it may be allowed to continue vibrating their souls.

The psychologist, the observer of souls, the person of broad practical experience, and the doctor thus all become a unity, insofar as the child is concerned. This is important, since anything that makes an impression on the child, anything that causes the soul's response, continues in the blood circulation and digestion, becoming a part of the foundation of health in later years. Due to the imitative nature of the child, whenever we educate the spirit and soul of the child, we also educate the body and physical nature of the child. This is the wonderful metamorphosis—that whatever approaches children, touching their spirit and soul, becomes their physical, organic organization, and their predisposition to health or illness in later life.

Consequently, we can say that if Waldorf schools educate out of spirit and soul, it is not because we choose to work in an unbalanced way with only the soul and spirit; rather, it is because we know that this is how we physically educate the inner being in the highest sense of the word. The physical being exists within the envelope of the skin.

Perhaps you recall yesterday's examples. Beginning with the model supplied by the human forces of heredity, the person builds a second human being, experienced in the second phase of life between the change of teeth and puberty. During the initial phase of life, human beings win for themselves a second being through what resulted of a purely spiritual life between death and rebirth. During the second stage of life, however, between the change of teeth and puberty, the influences of the outer world struggle with what must be incorporated into the individuality of the human being.

During this second stage, external influences grow more powerful. The inner human being is strengthened, however, since at this point it no longer allows every influence in the environment to continue vibrating in the body organization as though it were mainly a sense organ. Sensory perception begins to be more concentrated at the surface, or periphery, of the being. The senses now become more individual and autonomous, and the first thing that appears in the human being is a way of relating to the world that is not intellectual but compares only to an artistic view of life.

The Teacher as Artist

Our initial approach to life had a religious quality in that we related to nature as naturally religious beings, surrendered to the world. In this second stage, however, we are no longer obligated to merely accept passively everything coming from our environment, allowing it to vibrate in us physically; rather, we transform it creatively into images. Between the change of teeth and puberty, children are artists, though in a childish way, just as in the first phase of life, children were *homo religiosus*— naturally religious human beings.

Now that the child demands everything in a creative, artistic way, the teachers and educators who encounter the child must present everything from the perspective of an artist. Our contemporary culture demands this of teachers, and this is what must flow into the art of education; at this point, interactions between the growing human being and educators must take an artistic form. In this respect, we face great obstacles as teachers. Our civilization and the culture all around us have reached the point where they are geared only to the intellect, not to the artistic nature.

Let us consider the most wonderful natural processes—the description of embryonic life, for example, as portrayed in modern textbooks, or as taught in schools. I am not criticizing them, merely describing them; I know very well that they had to become the way they are and were necessary at a certain point in evolution. If we accept what they offer from the perspective of the spiritual force ready to reawaken today, something happens in our feeling life that we find impossible to acknowledge, because it seems to be a sin against the maturity attained by humanity in world-historical evolution. Difficult as it may be, it would be a good thing if people were clear about this.

When we read modern books on embryology, botany, or zoology, we feel a sense of despair in finding ourselves immediately forced to plunge into a cold intellectuality. Although the life and the development of nature are not essentially "intellectual," we have to deliberately and consciously set aside every artistic element. Once we have read a book on botany written according to strict scientific rules, our first task as teachers is to rid ourselves of everything we found there. Obviously, we must assimilate the information about botanical processes, and the sacrifice of learning from such books is necessary; but in order to educate children between the change of teeth and puberty, we must eliminate what we found there, transforming everything into artistic, imaginal forms through our own artistic activity and sensibility. Whatever lives in our thoughts about nature must fly on the wings of artistic inspiration and transform into images. They must rise in the soul of the child.

Artistically shaping our instruction for children between the change of teeth and puberty is all that we should be concerned with in the metamorphosis of education for our time and the near future. If the first period of childhood requires a priestly element in education, the second requires an artistic element. What are we really doing when we educate a person in the second stage of life? The I-being journeying from an earlier earthly life and from the spiritual world is trying gradually to develop and permeate a second human being. Our job is to assist in this process; we incorporate what we do with the child as teachers into the forces that interwove with spirit and soul to shape the second being with a unique and individual character. Again, the consciousness of this cosmic context must act as an enlivening impulse, running through our teaching methods and the everyday conditions of education. We cannot contrive what needs to be done; we can only allow it to happen through the influence of the children themselves on their teachers.

Two extremes must be avoided. One is a result of intellectualizing tendencies, where we approach children in an academic way, expecting them to assimilate sharply outlined ideas and definitions. It is, after all, very comfortable to instruct and teach by definitions. And the more gifted children learn to parrot them, allowing the teacher to be certain that they retain what has been taught them in the previous lesson, whereas those who don't learn can be left behind.

Such methods are very convenient. But it's like a cobbler who thinks that the shoes made for a three-year-old girl should still fit the ten-year-old, whereas only her toes fit into the shoes but not the heels. Much of a child's spiritual and psychic nature is ignored by the education we give children. It is necessary that, through the medium of flexible and artistic forms, we give children perceptions, ideas, and feelings in pictorial form that can metamorphose and grow with the soul, because the soul itself is growing. But before this can happen, there must be a living relationship between child and teacher, not the dead relationship that arises from lifeless educational concepts. Thus, all instruction given to children between approximately seven and fifteen must be permeated with pictures.

In many ways, this runs counter to the ordinary tendencies of modern culture, and we of course belong to this modern culture. We read books that impart much significant substance through little squiggles we call *a*, *b*, *c*, and so on. We fail to realize that we have been damaged by being forced to learn these symbols, since they have absolutely no relationship to our inner life. Why should *a* or *b* look the way they do today? There is no inner necessity, no experience that justifies writing an *h* after an *a* to express a feeling of astonishment or wonder.

This was not always the situation, however. People first made images in pictographic writing to describe external processes, and when they looked at the sheet or a board on which something had been written, they received an echo of that outer object or process. In other words, we should spare the child of six or seven from learning to write as it is done today. What we need instead is to bring the child something that can actually arise from the child's own being, from the activities of his or her arms and fingers. The child sees a shining, radiant object and receives an impression; we then fix it with a drawing that represents the impression of radiance, which a child can understand.

If a child strokes a stick from top to bottom and then makes a stroke on the paper from top to bottom, the meaning is obvious. I show a fish to a child, who then follows the general direction of the form, followed by the front and back fins that cross in the opposite direction. I draw the general form of the fish, and this line across it, and say to the child, "Here, on the paper, you have something like a fish." Then I go into the child's inner experience of the fish. It contains an *f*, and so I draw a line crossed by another line, and thus, out of the child's feeling experience, I have a picture that corresponds to the sound that begins the word *fish*. All writing can be developed in this way—not a mere copying of the abstract now in use, but a perception of the things themselves as they arise from a child's drawing and painting. When I derive writing from the drawing and painting, I am working with the living forces of an image.

It would be enough to present the beginning of this artistic approach; we can feel how it calls on the child's whole being, not just an intellectual understanding, which is overtaxed to a certain extent. If we abandon the intellectual element for imagery at this age, the intellect usually withdraws into the background. If, on the other hand, we overemphasize the intellect and are unable to move into a mode of imagery, the child's breathing process is delicately and subtly disrupted. The child can become congested, as it were, with weakened exhalation. You should think of this as very subtle, not necessarily obvious. If education is too intellectual between the ages of seven and fourteen, exhalation becomes congested, and the child is subjected to a kind of subconscious nightmare. A kind of intimate nightmare arises, which becomes chronic in the organism and leads in later life to asthmas and other diseases connected with swelling in the breathing system.

Another extreme occurs when the teacher enters the school like a little Caesar, with the self-image of a *mighty* Caesar, of course. In this situation, the child is always at the mercy of a teacher's impulsiveness. Whereas extreme intellectualism leads to congested exhalation, the metabolic forces are thinned by overly domineering and exaggerated assertiveness in the teacher. A child's digestive organs are gradually weakened, which again may have chronic effects in later life. Both of these excesses must be eliminated from education—too much intellectualizing and extreme obstinateness.

We can hold a balance between the two by what happens in the soul when we allow the will to pass gently into the child's own activity and by toning down the intellect so that feelings are cultivated in a way that does not suppress the breathing, but cultivates feelings that turn toward imagery and express the buoyant capacity I described. When this is done, the child's development is supported between the change of teeth and puberty.

Thus, from week to week, month to month, year to year, a true knowledge of the human being will help us read the developing being like a book that tells us what needs to be done in the teaching. The curriculum must reproduce what we read in the evolutionary process of the human being. Specific ways that we can do this will be addressed in coming lectures.

Lecture Three

Before education can be helpful, teachers and educators must gain the right perspective, one that allows them to fully understand the source and the formation of a child's organism. For the sake of clarity in this area I would like to begin with a comparison.

Let's take reading—the ordinary reading of adults. If we wanted to describe what we gain from our usual reading of a book, we would not say, "the letter *B* is shaped like this, the letter *C* like that" and so on. If I read Goethe's *Wilhelm Meister*, it wouldn't occur to me to describe the individual letters as a result of my reading, since the real substance assimilated is not on the paper at all, it's not even contained within the covers of the book. Nevertheless, if I want to comprehend in any way the content of *Wilhelm Meister*, I would have had to have learned how to read the letters and their relationships—I must be able to recognize the forms of the letters.

The Ability to Read the Human Being

A teacher's relationship with children is similar; it must constitute a reading of the human being. What a teacher gets from a strictly physical understanding of the physiology and anatomy of the organs and their functions amounts to no more than learning the letters. As teachers and educators, it is not enough to understand that the lungs or heart have this or that appearance and function in the physical realm; that kind of an understanding of the human being is similar an to illiterate person who can only describe the forms of letters but not the book's meaning.

Now in the course of modern civilization, humankind has gradually lost the habit of reading nature and, most of all, human nature. Our natural science is not reading but mere spelling. As long as we fail to recognize this specifically, we can never develop a true art of education that arises from real knowledge of the human being. This requires knowledge that truly reads, not one that only spells. People are obviously unhappy at first when they hear such a statement, and it is left at that. They argue: Isn't the human race supposed to be making continual progress? How can it be, then, that during our time of momentous progress in the natural sciences (which philosophical anthroposophists are the first to acknowledge) we are moving backward in terms of penetrating the world more deeply?

We must answer: Until the fourteenth or fifteenth century, human beings were unable to "spell out" nature. They saw natural phenomena and received instinctive, intuitive impressions, primarily from other human beings. They did not get as far as describing separate organs, but their culture was spiritual and sensible, and they had an instinctive impression of the human being as a totality. This kind of impression only arises when one is not completely free in one's inner being, since it is an involuntary impression and not subject to inner control.

Thus, beginning with the fourteenth or fifteenth century, a time had to come in the historical evolution of humanity—an epoch of world history that is about to end—when human beings would forgot their earlier, instinctive knowledge, and become more concerned with learning the "alphabet" of human nature. Consequently, in the last third of the nineteenth century and, in effect, until the present period of the twentieth century, as human beings we were faced with a larger culture whose worldview is void of spirit. This is similar to the way we would face a spiritual void if we could not read, but only perceived the forms of the letters. In this age, human nature in general has been strengthened, just because the involuntary life and being of the spirit within it were absent, especially among the educated.

We must have the capacity to observe world history in depth, since otherwise we would be incapable of forming a correct assessment of our position as human beings in the sequence of eras. In many ways, modern people will be averse to this, because we are endowed, as I have already indicated, with a certain cultural pride, especially when we think we have learned something. We place an intrinsically higher value on a "letter" reading of nature than we do on what existed in earlier periods of earthly evolution. Of course, anatomists today think they know more about the heart and liver than those of earlier times. Nevertheless, people then had a picture of the heart and liver, and their perception included a spiritual element.

We must be able to empathize with the way the modern anatomist views the heart, for example. It is seen as something like a first-rate machine—a more highly developed pump that drives the blood through the body. If we say that an anatomist is looking at a corpse, the response would be denial, which from that viewpoint is appropriate, since an anatomist wouldn't see the point of such a distinction. Ancient anatomists, however, saw a kind of spiritual entity in the heart, working in a spiritual and psychic sense. The sensory content of perception was permeated and simultaneous with a spiritual aspect. Such perception of the spiritual could not be fully clear and conscious, but was involuntary. If humankind had been forced to continue to experience a simultaneous revelation of spirit in sense perception, complete moral freedom could not have been attained. Nevertheless, at some point it had to enter historical evolution.

When we go back over the whole course of history since the fourteenth century, we find a universal struggle toward freedom, which was ultimately expressed in the revolutionary movements of the eighteenth century (particularly in the widespread fermentation in the more developed regions, beginning with the Bohemian-Magyar brotherhoods in Central Europe, where a definite pedagogic impulse was trying to make itself felt) and onward to Wycliffe, Huss, and the so-called Reformation. This struggle of humanity for the inner experience of freedom still continues.

None of this could have happened while the old perceptual mode persisted. Human beings had to be liberated for a while from the spirit working involuntarily within them so that they could freely assume that spirit itself. An unbiased observation of the activity of spiritual culture leads one to say: It is of primary importance that educators develop full awareness of the process of human evolution on Earth. Whereas there used to be an unconscious bond between teacher and student—which was true of ancient times—they must now develop a conscious bond. This is not possible if culture arises from mere spelling, which is the way of all science and human cognition today. Such a conscious relationship can arise only if we learn to progress consciously from spelling to reading. In other words, in the same way we grasp the letters in a book but get something very different from what the letters say (indeed, the letters themselves are innocent in terms of the meaning of *Wilhelm Meister*), so we must also get from human nature something that modern natural science cannot express by itself; it is acquired only when we understand the statements of natural science as though they were letters of an alphabet, and thus we learn to read the human being.

This explains why it is not correct to say that anthroposophic knowledge disregards natural science. This is not true. Anthroposophic knowledge gives a great deal of credit to natural science, but like someone who respects a book through the desire to read it, rather than one who merely wants to photograph the forms of the letters. When we try to truly describe the culture of our time, many interesting things can be said of it. If I give someone a copy of *Wilhelm Meister*, there is a difference between someone wanting to quickly get a camera to photograph every page, not bothering at all about the content of the book, and someone else who longs to know what the book is about. If I can be content with only natural science to help me understand the human being, I am like the first person—all I really want is photographs of the external forms, since the available concepts allow no more than a mere photograph of the forms.

We are forced to use radical expressions to describe the relationship that people today have with one another and with the world. This relationship is completely misunderstood. The belief is that human beings really have something higher today than was available before the fourteenth century; but this is not true. We must develop to the degree that we learn to manipulate consciously, freely, and deliberately what we have, just as in earlier times we gained our concepts of human nature through instinctive intuition. This development in modern culture should pass through teacher training education like a magic breath and become a habit of the soul in the teachers, since only it can place the teachers at the center of that horizon of worldview, which they should perceive and survey.

Thus, today it is not as necessary that people take up a scientific study of memory, will, and intelligence. It is more important that pedagogical and didactic training be directed toward evoking the attitude I described within the teachers' souls. The primary focus of a teacher's training should be the very heart of human nature itself. When this is the situation, every experience of a teacher's development will be more than lifeless pedagogical rules; they will not need to ponder the application of one rule or another to a child standing in front of them, which would be fundamentally wrong.

An intense impression of the child as a whole being must arise within the whole human nature of the teacher, and what is perceived in the child must awaken joy and vitality. This same joyful and enlivening spirit in the teacher must be able to grow and develop until it becomes direct inspiration in answer to the question: What must I do with this child? We must progress from reading human nature in general to reading an individual human being. Everywhere education must learn to manipulate (pardon this rather materialistic expression) what is needed by the human being. When we read, what we have learned about the relationships between the letters is applied. A similar relationship must exist between teacher and pupils. Teachers will not place too much nor too little value on the material development of the bodily nature; they will adopt the appropriate attitude toward bodily nature and then learn to apply what physiology and experimental psychology have to say about children. Most of all, they will be able to rise from a perception of details to a complete understanding of the growing human being.

The Implications of the Change of Teeth

A deeper perception reveals that, at the elementary school age, children are fundamentally different after their change of teeth. Let's look into the nature of the human being before the change of teeth. The teeth are the outer expression of something developing within the human organism as a whole (as I described yesterday). There is a "shooting up" into form—the human soul is working on the second bodily nature, like a sculptor working at shaping the material. An inner, unconscious shaping process is in fact happening. The only way this can be influenced externally is to allow children to imitate what we do. Anything I do—any movement I make with my own hand—passes into the children's soul building processes when they perceive it, and my hand movement causes an unconscious shaping activity that "shoots up" into the form.

This process depends completely on the element of movement in the child. Children make movements, their will impulses change from chaotic irregularity into inner order, and they work on themselves sculpturally from without. This plastic activity largely moves toward the inner being. When we meet children at the elementary age, we should realize that in the development of their spirit, soul, and body, the process that initially lived only in the movements passes into a very different region. Until the change of teeth, blood formation in the child depends on the system in the head. Think of a human being during the embryonic period, how the head formation dominates, while the rest of the organic structuring depends on external processes; regardless of what takes place in the mother's body, everything that proceeds from the baby itself begins with the formation of the head. This is still true, though less so, during the first period of life until the change of teeth. The head formation plays an essential role in all that happens within the human organism. The forces coming from the head, nerves, and sensory system all work into the motor system and the shaping activity. After the child passes through the change of teeth, the activities of the head move to the background. What works in the limbs now depends less on the head and more on the substances and forces passing into the human organism through nourishment from outside.

I would like you to consider this carefully. Suppose that, before the change of teeth, we eat some cabbage, for example. The cabbage contains certain forces intrinsic to cabbages, which play an important part in the way it grows in the field. Now, in the child those forces are driven out of the cabbage as quickly as possible by the process of digestion being carried on by forces that flow down from the child's head. Those forces flow from the head of the child and immediately plunge into the forces contained in the vegetable. After the change of teeth, the vegetable retains its own forces for a much longer time on its way through the human organism; the first transformation does not occur in the digestive system at all, but only where the digestive system enters the circulatory system. The transformation takes place later, and consequently, a completely different inner life is evoked within the organism. During the first years before the change of teeth, everything really depends on the head formation and its forces; the important thing for the second life stage from the change of teeth until puberty is the breathing process and meeting between its rhythm and the blood circulation. The transformation of these forces at the boundary between the breathing process and the circulatory system is particularly important. The essential thing, therefore, during the elementary school age, is that there should always be a certain harmony—a harmony that must be furthered by the education—between the rhythm developed in the breathing system and the rhythm it encounters in the interior of the organism. This rhythm within the circulatory system springs from the nourishment taken in. This balance—the harmonization of the blood system and the breathing system—is brought about in the stage between the change of teeth and puberty.

In an adult, the pulse averages four times as many beats as breaths per minute. This normal relationship in the human organism between the breathing and the blood rhythms is established during the time between the change of teeth and puberty. All education at that time must be arranged so that the relationship between the breathing and blood rhythms may be established in a way appropriate to the majesty and development of the human organism.

This relationship between pulse and breath always differs somewhat among people. It depends in each individual on the person's size, or whether one is thin or fat; it is influenced by the inner growth forces and by the shaping forces that still emanate from hereditary conditions during the early years of childhood. Everything depends on each human being having a relationship between the breathing and the blood rhythms suited to one's size and proportions. When I see a child who is inclined to grow up thin, I recognize the presence of a breathing system that, in a certain sense, affects the blood system more feebly than in some fat little child before me. In the thin child, I must strengthen and quicken the imprint of the breathing rhythm to establish the proper relationship. All these things, however, must work naturally and unconsciously in the teacher, just as perception of individual letters is unconscious once we know how to read. We must acquire a feeling of what should be done with a fat child or with a thin child, and so on. It is, for example, extremely important to know whether a child's head is large or small in proportion to the rest of the body. All this follows naturally, however, when we stand in the class with an inner joy toward education as a true educational individual, and when we can read the individual children committed to our care.

It is essential, therefore, that we take hold, as it were, of the continual shaping process—a kind of further development of what takes place until the change of teeth—and meet it with something that proceeds from the breathing rhythm. This can be done with various music and speech activities. The way we teach the child to speak and the way we introduce a child to the music—whether listening, singing, or playing music—all serve, in terms of teaching, to form the breathing rhythm. Thus, when it meets the rhythm of the pulse, it can increasingly harmonize with it.

It is wonderful when the teacher can observe the changing facial expressions of a child while learning to speak and sing— regardless of the delicacy and subtlety of those changes, which may not be so obvious. We should learn to observe, in children between the change of teeth and puberty, their efforts at learning to speak and sing, their gaze, physiognomy, finger movements, stance and gait; with reverence, we should observe, growing from the very center of very small children, unformed facial features that assume a beautiful form; we should observe how our actions around small children are translated into their developing expressions and body gestures. When we can see all this with inner reverence, as teachers we attain something that continually springs from uncharted depths, an answer in feeling to a feeling question.

The question that arises—which need not come into the conscious intellect—is this: What happens to all that I do while teaching a child to speak or sing? The child's answer is: "I receive it," or, "I reject it." In body gestures, physiognomy, and facial expressions we see whether what we do enters and affects the child, or if it disappears into thin air, passing through the child as though nothing were assimilated. Much more important than knowing all the rules of teaching—that this or that must be done in a certain way—is acquiring this sensitivity toward the child's reflexes, and an ability to observe the child's reactions to what we do. It is, therefore, an essential intuitive quality that must develop in the teacher's relationship with the children. Teachers must also learn to read the effects of their own activity. Once this is fully appreciated, people will recognize the tremendous importance of introducing music in the right way into education during the elementary years and truly understand what music is for the human being.

Understanding the Fourfold Human Being

Anthroposophy describes the human physical body, a coarse, material principle, and the more delicate body, which is still material but without gravity—in fact, its tendency is to fly against gravity into cosmic space. The human being has a heavy physical body, which can fall to the ground when not held upright. We also have a finer etheric body, which tends to escape gravity into cosmic space. Just as the physical body falls if it is unsupported, so the etheric body must be controlled by inner forces of the human organism to prevent it from flying away. Therefore, we speak of the physical body, the etheric body, and then the astral body, which is no longer material but spiritual; and we speak of the I-being, which alone is completely spirit. If we want to gain a real knowledge of these four members of the human being—a true understanding of the human being—we might say: The methods of modern anatomy and physiology allow for an understanding of the physical organism, but not the etheric human being and certainly not the astral human being.

How can we understand the etheric body? This requires a much better preparation than is usual for understanding the human being today. We understand the etheric body when we enter the shaping process, when we know how a curve or angle grows from inner forces. We cannot understand the etheric body in terms of ordinary natural laws, but through our experience of the hand—the spirit permeated hand. Thus, there should be no teacher training without activities in the areas of modeling or sculpture, an activity that arises from the inner human being. When this element is absent, it is much more harmful to education than not knowing the capital city of Romania or Turkey, or the name of some mountain; those things can always be researched in a dictionary. It is not at all necessary to know the masses of matter required for exams; what is the harm in referring to a dictionary? However, no dictionary can give us the flexibility, the capable knowledge, and knowing capacity necessary to understand the etheric body, because the etheric body does not arise according to natural laws; it permeates the human being in the activity of shaping.

And we shall never understand the astral body simply by knowing Gay-Lussac's law or the laws of acoustics and optics.[1] The astral body is not accessible to such abstract, empirical laws; what lives and weaves within it cannot be perceived by such methods. If we have an inner understanding, however, of the intervals of the third or the fifth, for example—an inner musical experience of the scale that depends on inner musical perception and not on acoustics—then we experience what lives in the astral human being.

The astral body is not natural history, natural science, or physics; it is *music*. This is true to the extent that, in the forming activity within the human organism, it is possible to trace how the astral body has a musical formative effect in the human being. This formative activity flows from the center between the shoulder blades, first into the tonic of the scale; as it flows on into the second, it builds the upper arm, and into the third, the lower arm. When we come to the third we arrive at the difference between major and minor; we find two bones in the lower arm—not just one—the radius and ulna, which represent minor and major. One who studies the outer human organization, insofar as it depends on the astral body, must approach physiology not as a physicist, but as a musician. We

1. Gay-Lussac's law refers to numerical ratios in the combination of gases.

must recognize the inner, formative music within the human organism.[2]

No matter how you trace the course of the nerves in the human organism, you will never understand what it means. But when you follow the course of the nerves musically— understanding the musical relationships (everything is audible here, though not physically)—and when you perceive with spiritual musical perception how these nerves run from the limbs toward the spine and then turn upward and continue toward the brain, you experience the most wonderful musical instrument, which is the human being, built by the astral body and played by the I-being.

As we ascend from there, we learn how the human being forms speech through understanding the inner configuration of speech—something that is no longer learned in our advanced civilization; it has discarded everything intuitive. Through the structure of speech, we recognize the I-being itself if we understand what happens when a person speaks the sound *"ah"* or *"ee"*—how in *"ah"* there is wonder, in *"ee"* there is a consolidation of the inner being; and if we learn how the speech element shoots, as it were, into the inner structure; and if we learn to perceive a word inwardly, not just saying, for example, that a rolling ball is "rolling," but understand what moves inwardly like a rolling ball when one says *"r o l l i n g."* We learn through inner perception—a perception really informed by the spirit of speech—to recognize what is active in speech.

These days, information about the human organism must come from physiologists and anatomists, and information about what lives in language comes from philologists. There is

---

2. This theme is discussed in considerable detail by Armin Husemann in *The Harmony of the Human Body: Musical Principles in Human Physiology*, Floris Books, Edinburgh, UK, 1989.

no relationship, however, between what they can say to each other. It is necessary to look for an inner spiritual connection; we must recognize that a genius of speech lives and works in language, a genius of speech that can be investigated. When we study the genius of speech, we recognize the human I-being.[3]

We have now made eurythmy part of our Waldorf education. What are we doing with eurythmy? We divide it into *tone* eurythmy and *speech* eurythmy. In tone eurythmy, we evoke in the child movements that correspond to the form of the astral body; in speech eurythmy we evoke movements that correspond to the child's I-being. We thus work consciously to develop the soul by bringing physical elements into play in tone eurythmy; and we work consciously to develop the spirit aspect by activating the corresponding physical elements in speech eurythmy.

Such activity, however, only arises from a complete understanding of the human organization. Those who think they can get close to the human being through external physiology and experimental psychology (which is really only another kind of physiology) would not recognize the difference between beating on a wooden tray and making music in trying to evoke a certain mood in someone. Similarly, knowledge must not remain stuck in abstract, logical rules, but rise to view human life as more than grasping lifeless nature—the living that has died—or thinking of the living in a lifeless way. When we rise from abstract principles to formative qualities and understand how every natural law molds itself sculpturally, we come to understand the human etheric body. When we begin to "hear" (in an inner, spiritual sense) the cosmic rhythm expressing itself in that most wonderful musical instrument that the astral body

---

3. See Rudolf Steiner, *The Genius of Language*, Anthroposophic Press, Hudson, NY, 1995 (GA 299).

makes of the human being, we come to understand the astral nature of the human being.

What we must become aware of may be expressed this way: First, we come to know the physical body in an abstract, logical sense. Then we turn to the sculptural formative activity with intuitive cognition and begin to understand the etheric body. Third, as a physiologist, one becomes a musician and views the human being the way one would look at a musical instrument—an organ or violin—where one sees music realized. Thus, we understand the astral human being. And when we come to know the genius of speech as it works creatively in words—not merely connecting it with words through the external memory—we gain knowledge of the human I-being.

These days, we would become a laughing stock if in the name of university reform—medical studies, for example—we said that such knowledge must arise from the study of sculpture, music, and speech. People would say: Sure, but how long would such training take? It certainly lasts long enough without these things. Nevertheless, the training would in fact be shorter, since its length today is due primarily to the fact that people don't move beyond abstract, logical, empirical sense perception. It's true that they begin by studying the physical body, but this cannot be understood by those methods. There is no end to it. One can study all kinds of things throughout life—there's no end to it—whereas study has its own inner limits when it is organically built up as a study of the organism in body, soul and spirit.

The point is not to map out a new chapter with the help of anthroposophy, adding to what we already have. Indeed, we can be satisfied with what ordinary science offers; we are not opposed to that. We are grateful to science in the sense that we are grateful to the violin maker for providing a violin. What we need in our culture is to get hold of all of this modern culture and permeate it with soul and permeate it with spirit, just as human beings themselves are permeated with soul and spirit. The artistic must not be allowed to exist in civilization as a pleasant luxury next to serious life, a luxury we consider an indulgence, even though we may have a spiritual approach to life in other ways. The artistic element must be made to permeate the world and the human being as a divine spiritual harmony of law.

We must understand how, in facing the world, we first approach it with logical concepts and ideas. The being of the universe, however, gives human nature something that emanates from the cosmic formative activity working down from the spheres, just as earthly gravity works up from the central point of the Earth. And cosmic music, working from the periphery, is also a part of this. Just as the shaping activity works from above, and physical activity works from below through gravity, so cosmic music works in the movements of the starry constellations at the periphery.

The principle that really gives *humanity* to the human being was divined in ancient times when words were spoken—words such as "In the primal beginning was the Word, and the Word was with God, and a God was the Word." That Cosmic Word, Cosmic Speech, is the principle that also permeates the human being, and that being becomes the I-being. In order to educate, we must acquire knowledge of the human being from knowledge of the cosmos, and learn to shape it artistically.

Lecture Four

Teaching Writing before Reading

This morning I attempted to describe the way knowledge itself must be transformed inwardly from mere knowledge about nature into higher forms of cognition. This allows our understanding of the whole human being and the growing child to be translated into an artistic approach to education and instruction. I can imagine that a certain question may arise: Assuming that a teacher thoroughly understands the physical body through pure observation and intellect, the etheric body through shaping activity, the astral body through the concept of music, and the I-being through insight into the true nature of speech, what practical application does this have?

Certainly, if we must describe education and instruction as a whole—as we have for Waldorf methods in these lectures—then we would have to say that the most important aspect of a teacher's perspective on life and the world is not what we generally understand as a "worldview"—that would be completely theoretical. Instead, it is an aspect that, as a soul force, can enter the whole activity of the human being. Any teacher who tries to acquire the principles of education from today's recognized knowledge of the human being would have to look elsewhere for the necessary inspiration. Hence the continual references to educational ideals that, however convincing they appear, always remain ineffective, because they are rooted in abstractions.

Nevertheless, true insight that penetrates the nature of the world and the human being will, by its very nature, enkindle inspiration in the human heart. While practicing their profession, teachers can always draw inspiration from the feeling of their relationship to the world and to their own being—like artists, whose work seems to live in their very marrow. The artist doesn't need to go anywhere else for inspiration—it comes from the thing itself. Similarly, the inspiration found by teachers in their worldview, experienced internally and constantly renewed, is carried into the soul constitution of the children entrusted to them. Such inspiration lives in everything the teacher does at school.

Those who have insight into the human being have the ability to perceive that a musical element flows into harmony with the formative processes in the inner being of the child during the elementary years, between the change of teeth and puberty. Such a person will never be likely to stray from the right way of teaching, writing, and reading to children. They have a living understanding that writing—particularly as described here— mobilizes the whole being; it uses the arms and hands and permeates them with spirit that exercises the whole person.

These are the very aspects of the human being that will be perceived in a living way if we begin with a view of the world such as I described this morning. It also helps to become clear that reading is merely a pursuit of the head, an unbalanced activity for the human being. The teacher will sense that such one-sidedness is suitable only for children whose whole being has become active. Thus, teachers who take hold of this insight into the human being will be careful to develop writing from painting and drawing (as I described) until children can write what they experience in their deepest being in words or sentences.

When children have reached a certain level of development, they can speak and then write what they have said. This is when it becomes appropriate to teach reading. Reading is easy to teach once writing has been somewhat developed. After children have begun work within their own being—in the nervous system and limbs, in the substance of their writing and reading, and in their inner participation in producing reading material—only then are they ready for one-sided activity. Then, without any danger to their development as human beings, the head can become active, and what they first learned by writing is turned into reading.

It really comes down to this: week after week and month after month, the germinating human being must be promoted to activity that suits the developing forces of the human organization. It is important to decide what should be done at each stage by reading the particular way each human being tries to evolve. It doesn't work to use schedules that limit some activity to an hour or forty-five minutes, then jump to something else, and again to a third lesson, and so on. Consequently, we have introduced a system of instruction into the Waldorf school where the same subject is taught during the early morning hours for several weeks at a time. In this approach to teaching—so-called "block" teaching, which is characteristic of Waldorf education—students immerse themselves in the subject; they are not torn away as soon as they meet it.

In everything that must be presented to children between the change of teeth and puberty we have to discover ways of reading what is needed through the demands of human nature itself. When it is a matter of gradually leading children into a real relationship to their own being and the world, it is most important that the teachers themselves have a real relationship to the world. In contemporary culture, of course, no matter how educated people may be, they cannot really acquire an inwardly alive and rich relationship to the world and their own being. This is yet another radical statement, but we must not be afraid of real insight into what must be gradually introduced into our civilization.

Understanding Cosmic Forces

Above all, it is necessary that the teachers themselves should not, in their own development, fall into what might be called a "cosmic parochialism," but rather look beyond what is strictly earthly and realize that, as human beings, they depend on nourishment not only from their immediate environment, but from the whole cosmos. Naturally, it is very difficult to speak of these things today in an unbiased way, since our culture offers little support for people's attempts to look beyond their dependence on the earthly elements. Consequently, old teachings emanating from earlier instinctive concepts are often carried into the present without any understanding, which leads to superstition. In reality, all that the modern mainstream culture can offer is no more than a kind of "cosmic parochialism," because this culture has not as yet produced ideas that would extend from Earth into the cosmos. We have calculations, or at least spectrum analysis, to teach us (or purport to teach us) about the course and position of the stars, their substance, and so on. Nevertheless, the intimate knowledge that comes from entering into a close relationship with the essential nature of the Earth cannot be acquired—in terms of the extraterrestrial cosmos—from the mainstream culture of today. The concepts that human beings formulate about such things as cabbage, spinach, venison, and so on, are completely different from those acquired through abstract, intellectual science. We eat those things, and abstract thought has nothing to do with eating! We do not eat to gain practical experience in what modern science tells us about the hare, for example; we get a much more concrete and intimate experience of it through taste and digestion.

In terms of the surrounding cosmos beyond Earth, our knowledge is such that we have no intimate relationships at all. If everything we knew about the hare were equivalent to what astronomy and spectrum analysis know about the extraterrestrial universe, and if we only knew the results of calculations of the relative positions of the bones and relative proportions of various substances within the hare, our relationship to it would be merely scientific; we would never find our way into any human relationship. It could never give us what the experienced human relationship to the hare can provide. People do not realize these days that in a more ancient, instinctive wisdom, people had an equally intimate relationship with the cosmos. If only they could acquire a true concept of that ancient wisdom, they would, at this more advanced stage of their soul's growth, again receive the impulse to look for a new wisdom in this area, a wisdom that can be as intimate in the human sense as the science of the natural objects in the earthly realm.

I would like to illustrate this with an example to show how important it is that teachers acquire a living relationship to the world. Teachers derive from that relationship the necessary enthusiasm to translate what should exist in the teacher's own soul into simple, visual pictures for the child. A teacher needs a truly consecrated relationship to the world. In the presence of the active child, this becomes the world of imagery that a child needs for help in progressing properly in harmony with the demands of human evolution. For example, we are surrounded by the world of plants; to ordinary sense-perception it presents many enigmas.

Goethe encountered many of these questions. He followed the growing plant forms in their various metamorphoses, and through observing the plants' growth he was led to a remarkable principle that pours new life into all our knowledge of the plant world. His principle may be described in this way: Let's begin by observing the seed, which we place in the ground and from which the plant grows. Seen from the outside, the life of the plant is compressed to a point in the seed. We then see the seed unfold, and life spreads out farther and farther, until it has fully unfolded in the first budding leaves. Then it contracts into the narrow channel of the stem, continues to the next leaf connection, and there it spreads out again, only to contract again into the stem toward the next leaf cluster, and so on. Eventually there is a final contraction when a new germ, or seed, is formed, and within that, the whole life of the plant again contracts to a single physical point. This is Goethe's contribution—how the growing plant shows an alternation: expansion, contraction, expansion, contraction.

Goethe looked deep into plant formation as an effluence of the plant's own life. However, the time was not ripe for him to relate to the world as a whole the formula he found for plant life, since the whole world and its forces are always involved in the ways any being lives and has its own being. With the help of contemporary spiritual science, or anthroposophic science, however, we now can extend Goethe's formula, as you can see for yourself in the spiritual scientific literature (and here I will only touch on this).

One will find there that what lives in the expansion of the plant's being is what comes from the Sun. The Sun is not merely what is described by astronomy and spectrum analysis; with the Sun's rays, spiritual forces stream and interweave down to the Earth. In this ensoulment of sunlight we have the element that, for example, determines expansion in the growth of the plant. It is not just that the Sun shines on the plant and causes it to expand; rather, the forces of growth in the plant itself have a sun-like quality that plants reflect back. On the other hand, whenever we witness contraction—whenever plant growth contracts back to a point in the passage from one leaf bud to the next, or in the formation of the seed—these are being influenced by the Moon's forces. Just as we see a rhythmic interchange of sunlight and moonlight in the cosmos, so we also see it reflected in the budding plant that responds to the activity of the Sun in the expansion of the leaves, and the Moon activity in the phenomena of contraction. Expansion and contraction in the plant are the reflected image of what pours down to Earth from cosmic, etheric space in an interchange of forces coming from Sun and Moon.

Here we have expanded our gaze from the Earth to etheric, cosmic spaces, and we get an impression of how the Earth, in a certain sense, nourishes her forces of fruitfulness and growth from what flows to her from the cosmos. We come to feel how, by making a detour through the plants, we grow together with the spirit of Sun and Moon. Here we are brought into contact with things that are usually left to the domain of calculation or spectrum analysis. The inspiration necessary for teaching growing children anything about humankind's relationship to the universe cannot be gotten from mere abstract observation—that a leaf is or isn't indented at its edges, or has this or that appearance. No inspiration will flow from this. Such inspiration does come, however, when the rhythmic reflection of Sun and Moon is revealed to us in the growth of various plants.

How wonderful the perception of surrounding nature becomes when we observe a plant that has a regular growth—for example, the buttercup. Here we find something sent up by the Earth as it surrenders itself lovingly to cosmic Sun and Moon forces, paying homage equally to both. Or look at a plant, such as the cactus, with its stalk portion widened out. What does this reveal? In the contraction manifested elsewhere by the stalk, we perceive Moon forces. When the stalk itself wants to expand, we see a struggle between Sun and Moon influences. The form of each plant reveals how Sun and Moon act together within it. Each individual plant is a "miniature world," a reflection of the greater world. Just as we see our own image in a mirror, in the mirror of growth on Earth, we see what is happening beyond in the cosmos.

Ancient, instinctive wisdom was conscious of such things, and what follows offers proof of this. In the plant life that buds from the Earth in spring, people saw a cosmic reflection of the relationship between Sun forces and Moon forces. Thus, spring was celebrated with the Easter festival, whose date was determined by the relationship between Sun and Moon. The Easter festival occurs on the first Sunday after the spring full moon. The time of the Easter festival is therefore determined in reference to the cosmos—the relationship between Sun and Moon. What people of those ancient times might have implied was this: When we see plants budding in spring, we are faced with the enigma of *why* they appear sometimes earlier and sometimes later. The fact that the time of the spring full moon plays an essential role in all these processes of budding and sprouting allows us to get to the heart of this riddle.

There are other factors, of course, but it is generally apparent that the interplay between Sun and Moon is expressed in what happens in spring, when one year the plants appear earlier and another, later. What might people say, however, if they acknowledge only parochial, scientific thinking about the Earth's dependence on the cosmos? They will say: The reason plants appear earlier in a particular year is due to less snow or because the snow melted more quickly; or that the delayed appearance of plants means that there was more snow. This is, of course, an easy explanation, but in fact it is not an explanation at all. Real insight comes only when we perceive that plant growth depends on the activity of Sun and Moon forces, and then go on to recognize that a shorter or longer duration of snow also depends on the Sun and Moon. The timing of the plants' appearance is determined by the same thing that determines the duration of the snow; the climatic and meteorological conditions in any given year are themselves subject to cosmic influences.

By continuing to develop these matters, we gain insights into the life of the Earth on her journey through the cosmos. We say that human beings thrive when there are plenty of cows, and they get a lot of milk, because we can point to the obvious human dependence on the immediate earthly environment. When we consider this connection, we are looking at human life from a nutritional perspective. Things come alive for us only when we perceive their relationship to their surroundings and how they transform what they receive from their environment.

When we behold the Earth wandering through cosmic space and taking into herself elements flowing from the Sun, Moon, and stars, we see the Earth as alive in the cosmos. We do not evolve a dead geology or geography but raise what these dead sciences have to offer into a description of the Earth's life in the cosmos; the Earth becomes a living being before our spiritual vision. In the plants springing from the Earth, we see the Earth reproducing what she received from the cosmos. The Earth and her plant growth become a unity; we realize what nonsense it is to tear a plant out of the Earth and then examine it from root to blossom, imagining that we are viewing reality. It is no more reality than a hair torn from a human head. The hair belongs to the whole organism, and it can be understood only as a part of the whole organism. To tear out a hair and study it in isolation is just as absurd as uprooting a plant to study it in isolation. The hair must be studied in connection with the human organism and the plant in connection with the whole living Earth.

In this way a person's own being is woven with the living Earth; an individual no longer goes around feeling subjected only to the Earth's forces, but also perceives in the environment what is working in from etheric distances. We have a living perception of the way forces from the cosmos are active everywhere—drawing the etheric body to themselves just as the physical body is drawn to the Earth. We then acquire a natural perception of the etheric body's tendency to pass into cosmic space, just as we sense gravity drawing our physical body down to Earth. Our vision continues to expand so that knowledge becomes inner life and can become truly effective. Having believed the Earth to be a lifeless body in the cosmos, such knowledge now gives life to her. We must return again to a living cognition, just as we still see the aftereffects in such things as the determination of Easter time. But such insight into the cosmos must result from consciously developed knowledge—not from the instinctive knowledge of earlier ages.

The Child's Need for Imagery in the Tenth Year

This cosmic insight lives in us in such a way that we can artistically shape it into the pictures we need. Someone who, when confronting the cosmos, sees the Sun and Moon determining all plant growth, feels the inspiration that can arise from these living intuitions; and that person's story of the plants is very different from the story of someone else who absorbs and elaborates the abstract concepts of modern texts on botany. The concept can grow rich in feeling and be communicated artistically to the child.

At around the tenth year, children are ready for what the teacher can make of this far-reaching vision. If one shows in living pictures how the Earth as a whole is a living being—how it has plants the way a person has hair, though in greater complexity—and if one builds a living unity between the living being Earth and the plants growing here or there, a kind of expansion occurs in the child's soul. Whenever we communicate something about the nature of the plants in this way, it is like bringing fresh air to someone who had been living until now in a stifling atmosphere—one can breathe freely in this fresh air. This expansion of the soul is the real result of this kind of knowledge—a knowledge that is truly equal to the task of understanding the mysteries of the universe.

Do not say that children are too immature for ideas such as this. Any teacher in whom these ideas are alive, and who is backed by this worldview, will know how to express them in ways children are prepared for, in ways that their whole being can agree with. Once such things are internalized by the teacher, the capacity to simplify them pictorially is also present, Whatever a teacher gives to the child must flow from this background, and thus a relationship between the child and the world is truly established. This leads the teacher to transform everything naturally into living pictures, since it simply becomes impossible to explain abstractly what I have said about the plant realm. The only way to convey this to children is to unfold it in vivid pictures, which appeal to the whole human being and not merely to the intellect.

You will quickly see the animation in children as they grasp something presented to them pictorially. They will not answer with a concept that merely comes from the lips—one that cannot be really formed yet—but they will tell a story using their arms and hands and all kinds of body language. Children will act in a way that uses the whole being; above all, these actions and signals will reveal the children's inner experience and their difficulty in understanding a subject. The best and most noble thing in acquiring knowledge is the feeling that it is difficult, that it costs effort to get hold of things. Those who imagine they can get to the heart of something—

insofar as it is necessary—merely through clever words have no reverence for the things of the world, and such reverence is a part of what makes a whole and perfect human being—to the degree that perfection is possible in earthly existence. The only way human beings can build a right relationship to the world is by feeling how helpless they are when they want to arrive at the real essence of things, and how the whole being must be brought into play. Only when the teacher has a proper relationship to the world can the child also establish one. *Pedagogy must be alive.* It involves more than just applying oneself; it must come to flower from the very life situations of education. And it can do this when it grows from the teachers' living experience of their own being in the cosmos.

The Human Being as a Symphony of the Tones in Animals

If musical understanding—which I mentioned this morning—has truly taught the teacher about the reality of the human astral body, providing a concept of the human being itself as a wonderful, inwardly organized musical instrument, such an understanding of the astral body will open an even broader understanding of the whole relation between the human being and the world. Naturally, this cannot be conveyed to children in the way I am going to express it, but it *can* be presented in pictures.

Teachers who have a knowledge of their own astral body, sounding inwardly in musical forms, should view the human being and the various animal forms that exist in the world. They can then understand the deep meaning contained in an old instinctual wisdom, which represented the human being as a coalescence of four beings—three lower and one higher: *lion, bull, eagle,* and *angel.* The bull represents an unbalanced development of the lowest forces of human nature. Picture the forces in the human metabolic-limb system without any balancing forces in the head and rhythmic systems; in other words, imagine an unbalanced and prevailing development of the metabolic-limb system. Here we have a one-sided formation that presents itself to us as the bull. We can thus imagine that if this bull nature were toned down by the human head organization, it would develop into something like the human being. If the central rhythmic system is developed in an unbalanced way—for example, through a contraction of the abdominal system or a stunting of the head system—we can picture it as lion nature.

If, however, there is one-sided development of the head organism in such a way that the forces otherwise existing in the inner part of the head push out into "feathers," we get a bird, or eagle nature. If we imagine forces that enable these three qualities to harmonize as a unity that can manifest by adding the angelic fourth, we get a synthesis of the three—the human being. This is a schematic way of presenting these things, but it shows our human relationship to the surrounding animal world. In this sense; human beings are not related just to the bull, eagle, and lion, but to all earthly animal forms. In each animal form we can find an unbalanced development of one of the organic systems of the human being. These things were alive in the instinctive wisdom of ancient times.

There was still a tradition in later times that was expressed paradoxically, because people themselves no longer had such vision but created intellectual elaborations of the old perceptions. In an odd passage, Oken asks us to suppose that the human tongue were developed in a one-sided way.[1] Actually, it is toned down, or moderated, by the forces of the head, because the tongue serves the stomach (regardless of its spatial distance

---

1. Lorenz Oken (1779–1851), German naturalist and philosopher. He attempted to unite the natural sciences; his work foreshadowed current theories of the cellular structure of organisms and the protoplasmic foundation of life.

from it), and so on. Suppose, however, that it were developed
one-sidedly. If a being were only tongue and all the rest only
appendage, what would the tongue be then—a cuttlefish; the
tongue is a cuttlefish! Now, of course, this is an exaggeration,
but it retains something of the ancient perception translated
into modern intellectualism. It is nonsense, but it originated
with something that once had deep meaning. The soul attitude
that underlies ancient knowledge can be rediscovered; we can
rediscover how to conceive of the human being as divided, as it
were, into all the various animal forms that exist on Earth. And
if we bring them all together—so that each is harmonized by
the others—we get the human being.

Thus, when we determine humankind's relationship to the
animal kingdom through observation, we find the relationship
between the astral body and the outer world. We must apply a
musical understanding to the astral body. I gaze into the
human being, and out toward the myriad animal forms. It's as
if we were to take a symphony where all the tones sound
together in a wonderful, harmonious, and melodious whole
and, over the course of time, separated each tone from the others and juxtaposed them.

As we look out into the animal world, we have the single
tones. As we look into the human astral body and what it
builds in the physical and etheric bodies, we have the symphony. If we go beyond an intellectual view of the world and
have enough cognitive freedom to rise to artistic knowledge,
we develop an inner reverence, permeated with religious fervor, for the invisible being—the marvelous world composer—
who first arranged the tones in the various animal forms, and
then created the human being as a symphony of the phenomena of animal nature. This is what we must carry in our souls
as teachers. If I understand my relationship to the world in
this way, a true enthusiasm in the presence of world creation

and world formation will flow into my descriptions of the animal forms. Every word and gesture in my teaching as a whole will be permeated by religious fervor—not just abstract concepts and natural laws.

Such things show us that instruction and education must not come from accumulated knowledge, which is then applied, but from a living abundance. A teacher comes into the class with the fullness of this abundance, and when dealing with children, it's as though they found before them a voice for the world mysteries pulsating and streaming through the teacher, as though merely an instrument through which the world speaks to the child. There is then a real inner, enlivening quality in the method of instruction, not just superficial pedantry. Enthusiasm must not be artificially produced, but blossom like a flower from the teacher's relationship to the world; this is the important thing.

In our discussion of a genuine method for teaching and the living foundations of education, we must speak of enthusiasm stimulated not by theoretical, abstract insight, but by true insight into the world. When we approach children who are between the change of teeth and puberty in this way, we can guide them in the right way toward puberty. As soon as puberty arrives, the astral body begins to unfold its independence. What was previously absorbed as the "music of the world" continues to develop within them. It is remarkable that the intellect now comprehends what has been developed in pictures and what was appropriated by the soul in an inwardly musical, sculptural sense and in living pictures during the period between the change of teeth and puberty. The human intellect does not absorb anything of what we force on it intellectually from outside; before the intellect can receive anything, it must first develop within the individual in a different way.

An important fact then comes into play. Something that one had all along is understood in an inwardly directed way—something that was prepared and supports puberty in the person who developed in a healthy way. All that was understood through images now arises from the inner wellspring. Proceeding to intellectual activity involves the human being looking into the self. I now take hold of my own being within myself and through myself. The astral body with its musical activity beats in rhythm with the etheric body with its shaping activity. In a healthy person, after puberty, a chord is sounded within the human being; it results in an awareness of one's self. And when there is this concordance between the two sides of an individual's nature, after puberty the person truly experiences inner freedom as a result of understanding for the first time what was merely perceived earlier.

The most important thing for which we can prepare a child is the experience of freedom, at the right moment in life, through the understanding of one's own being. True freedom is an inward experience and is developed only when the human being is viewed in this way. As a teacher, I must say that I cannot pass on freedom to another human being—each must experience it individually. Nevertheless, I must plant something within the person—something *intact* because I have left it untouched—to which that person's own intact being feels attracted and into which it may become immersed. This is the wonderful thing I have accomplished. I have educated within the human being what must be educated. In reverence to the Godhead in every individual human being, I have left untouched those things that may only be taken hold of by the self. I educate everything in the human being except what belongs to the self, and then I wait for it to take hold of what I have invoked. I do not coarsely handle the development of the human I, but prepare the soil for its development, which takes hold after puberty.

If I educate intellectually before puberty—if I offer abstract concepts or ready-made, sharply outlined observations instead of growing, living pictures—I am violating the human being and crudely handling the I within. I truly educate only when I leave the I untouched and wait until it can grasp what I have prepared through education. In this way, together with the child, I look forward to a time when I can say, "Here the I is being born in freedom; I have only prepared the ground so that the I may become conscious of its own being.

If I have educated the child this way until puberty, I find before me a human being who may say, "When I was not yet fully human, you gave me something that, now that it is possible, enables me to become fully human myself." In other words, I have educated so that, with every look, every movement, the human being says to me, "You have accomplished something with me; and my freedom has been left whole. You have made it possible for me to grant myself my own freedom at the right moment in life. You have done something that enables me to stand before you now, shaping myself as a human being from my individuality, which you left reverently untouched."

This may never be said in so many words, but it lives, nonetheless, in the human being who has received the right kind of education during the elementary school years.

The next lecture will show that there is much more to be done so that education and teaching may accommodate what the human being encounters after puberty.

Lecture Five

STUTTGART, APRIL 11, 1924

Living Education

In these five lectures my task has been to describe briefly some guidelines for Waldorf education. Here I have not tried to get into details but describe the spirit of this method as a whole, which should flow from anthroposophy. Perhaps even more than details—though they may be important—contemporary humanity needs a complete renewal and strengthening of all spiritual life. Aside from the spiritual substance that is of course necessary, all spiritual callings require a renewed enthusiasm that springs from knowledge of the world—a worldview that has been taken hold of in spirit. Today it is becoming obvious to a wide range of people that teachers—who must be soul-artists—need such enthusiasm more than anyone else. Perhaps people seek along paths that cannot lead to the goal, because people everywhere continue to fear a thorough investigation of spiritual matters. We base our educational method on the discovery of a teaching method—conditions that will make education viable through reading human nature itself; such reading will gradually reveal the human being so that we can adjust our education to what is revealed to every step of the curriculum and schedule.

Let's for a moment go into the spirit of how we read the human being. We have seen that children are naturally completely open—in a religious attitude, as it were—to their immediate human surroundings; they are imitative beings, and they elaborate in themselves through will-imbued perception all that they experience unconsciously and subconsciously from their environment. Children's bodily nature has a religious disposition, from the moment of entering the world until the change of teeth—of course, not in terms of substance, but in its constitution as a whole. The soul is initially spirit, which reveals itself outwardly as a natural creation. Human beings do not enter the world without predispositions—they do not arrive only with the physical forces of heredity from their ancestors but with forces individually brought from a previous earthly life. Consequently, they may at first be equally open to beauty and ugliness, to good and evil, to wisdom and foolishness, to skillfulness and unskillfulness. Our task, therefore, is to work around children—to the degree that we control our very thoughts and feelings—so that children may become beings who imitate goodness, truth, beauty, and wisdom.

When we think in this way, life flows into our interactions with children; education very obviously becomes a part of that life through our interactions with them. Education, therefore, is not something we work at in isolated activities, but something lived. Children develop in the right way in their growth to adulthood only when education is *lived with* children and not forced on them.

Morality and the Child's Natural Religious Feeling

What we have educated in children very naturally in a priestly way—what is really a religious devotion—we must now be able to reawaken at a higher soul level during the second stage of life, between the change of teeth and puberty. We do this by transforming pictorially everything we bring them, by transforming education into an artistic activity; nevertheless, it is a truly subjective and objective human activity. We educate children so that, through their relationship to the teacher, they are devoted aesthetically to beauty and internalize the images. Now it becomes essential that, in place of the religious element, a naturally *artistic* response to the world arises. This naturally artistic human attitude (which must not be confused with the treatment of "art as a luxury," which is so much a part of our civilization) includes what now would be seen as a *moral* relationship to the world.

When understood correctly, we realize that we will not get anything from children between the change of teeth and puberty by giving them rules. Prior to the change of teeth, moralizing won't get us anywhere with children; moralizing is inaccessible to a child's soul during the first period of life. Only the morality of our actions have access at that age—that is, the moral element children see expressed in the actions, gestures, thoughts, and feelings of those around them. Even during the second period of life—between the change of teeth and puberty—moralistic rules will not get us very close to a child. Children have no inner relationship to what is contained in moral commands. To them, they are only empty sounds.

We get close to children during this stage of life only by placing them in the context of natural authority. Children who cannot yet understand abstractly beauty, truth, goodness, and so on may develop this impulse through a sense that the teacher acts as the incarnation of goodness, truth, and beauty. When we understand children correctly, we understand that they have not gained any abstract, intellectual understanding for the revelations of wisdom, beauty, and goodness.

Nevertheless, children see what lives in the teacher's gestures, and they hear something revealed in how the teacher's words are spoken. It is the teacher whom the child calls—without saying it—truth, beauty, and goodness as revealed in the heart. And this is the way it must be.

When a teacher corresponds to what the child needs at this age, two things gradually grow in the child. The first is an inner aesthetic sense of pleasure and displeasure in the moral realm. Goodness pleases children when our whole personality exemplifies it. We must plan education so that the natural need to take pleasure in goodness can develop—and, likewise, displeasure in evil. How do children ask questions? Children do not ask intellectually with words, but deep in their hearts. "May I do this?" or, "May I do that?" They will be answered, "Yes, you may," if the teacher does it. "Should I leave this undone?" "Yes, because my teacher shows that it may be left undone."

This is how children experience the world through the teacher—the world as goodness or evil, as beauty or ugliness, and as truth or falsehood. This relationship to the teacher—the activity of the hidden forces between the child's heart and that of the teacher—is the most important aspect of the teaching method; the conditions for life in education are contained in this.

This is how pleasure in morality and displeasure in immorality should develop between the change of teeth and puberty. Then, however, something appears in the background of that growing moral feeling. What first existed naturally during the first period of the child's life—as a religious surrender to the environment—is resurrected, as it were, in a different form in this moral development; and, if the teacher's soul forces are equal to it, it is easy to relate what arises as pleasure in good and displeasure in evil to what flows as soul through the manifestations of nature. First a child is surrendered naturally to nature itself; since the moral element in the environment is perceived as a part of nature, a moral gesture is felt, imitated and made part of the child's being. But as we unfold the child's sense of pleasure in the good, this religious and natural attitude is transformed into a soul quality.

Now consider what this means. Until the change of teeth, through the magic of completely unconscious processes, we allow the child's religious attitude to develop naturally, through pure imitation; thus, we ground the religious element while we cannot yet touch the force of the inner, free individuality. We educate through nature and do not interfere with the soul and spirit. And when we approach the soul element between the change of teeth and puberty—since it is then that we must approach it—we do not force a religious feeling but awaken the child, and thus evoke the I in the human being.

In this way, we are already practical philosophers of freedom, since we do not say: You must believe this or that of the spirit; rather, we awaken innate human beliefs. We become awakeners, not stuffers of the souls of children. This constitutes the true reverence we must have for all creatures placed in the world by the Godhead, and we owe this especially to the human being. And thus we see how the I arises in the human being, and how moral pleasure and displeasure assume a religious quality.

Teachers who learn to observe what was initially a purely natural religious aspect as it strives toward transformation in the soul, embody through their words something that becomes a pleasing image of goodness, beauty, and truth. The child hangs on to something in the adult's words. Teachers and educators are still active in this, but their methods no longer appeal only to imitation but to something that exists behind imitation. It no longer stimulates outer bodily nature but the soul element. A religious atmosphere permeates moral pleasure and displeasure.

The Intellect after Puberty

The intellect becomes active in its own way once children reach puberty. Because of this, I have suggested that it is actually a matter of bringing human beings to the point where they

find within themselves what they must understand—draw
from their own inner being what was initially given as spontaneous imitation, then as artistic, imaginative activity. Thus,
even during the later period, we should not force things on the
human being so that there is the least feeling of arbitrary, logical compulsion.

It was certainly a great moment in the development of spiritual life in Germany when—specifically in reference to moral
experience—Schiller opposed Kant's concept of morality.
When Kant said, "Duty, you sublime and powerful name—
you who bear no enticements but demand stern submission,"
Schiller stood against it. He opposed this concept of duty,
which does not allow morality to arise from goodwill but only
from subjection. Schiller replied to Kant's idea of duty with the
remarkable words containing a true moral motto: "I willingly
serve my friend, but unfortunately I serve him from inclination; alas, I therefore lack virtue!"

Indeed, moral life as a whole arises from human nature in
purity only when duty becomes a deep human inclination,
when it becomes, in the words of Goethe, "*Duty*—that is,
where people love what they tell themselves to do." It was a
great moment when morality was purged of Kant's influence
and made human again through Schiller and Goethe.

What came at that time from German spiritual life nevertheless became immersed in nineteenth-century materialism, as it
still is today. Something appeared in civilization because we
forgot this powerful action in the moral realm, and our task is
now to raise humanity out of it. This rehabilitation of the
human being as a fully human and moral being is the special
task of those who have to teach and educate. In this consciousness, the impulse of living education will be able to arise. We
may say that the sun of German spiritual life shining in Schiller
and Goethe in the moral sphere should shine down especially

in the actions of those teachers and educators of the present who understand the task of this their own age, and who seek to develop through education a really human relationship of human beings to their own being and to the real needs of the civilization of the age. The task of this educational conference was to speak of the position of education in regard to human individuality and the culture of the age. We shall only accomplish this task if we can think with gratitude of the impulses that flowed into the evolution of Central Europe through great and shining spirits like Goethe and Schiller. When we seek to comprehend our true situation in the world, it is not merely in order to develop a critical sense, but above all things a gratitude for what has already been accomplished by human beings before us.

One could say, of course, that self-education should refer only to the education people give themselves. However, all education is self-education, not just in this subjective sense, but in an objective sense as well—in other words, educating the self of another. To educate (*erziehen*) means to "draw out," and it is related to "drawing" (*ziehen*).[1] The essence of what we invoke is left untouched. We do not smash a stone in order to pull it out of the water. Education does not demand that we in any way injure or overpower those who have entered the world; on the contrary, we must guide them to experience particularly the stage of culture reached by humanity as a whole when it descended from the divine-spiritual worlds into the sensible world. All these ideas, felt and experienced, are a part of the teaching method. The people who least understand the situation of education in our time are those in whom such ideas do not live.

---

1. The word *education* is believed to derive from *educere* (Latin) and *educe* (fifteenth-century English), meaning to "lead out" (also the source of *duct* and *duke*).

In the moral realm we allow pleasure in the good and displeasure in the evil to grow; we allow the religious element, which was originally natural in the child, to awaken in the soul. In the depths, however, between the change of teeth and puberty there develops the seed and foundation—something already was present—that becomes free understanding after the age of puberty. We prepare a free understanding of the world that includes the religious and moral spheres. It is great when a person can recognize how pleasure and displeasure were experienced as a permeation of the whole life of feeling as the moral qualities of good and evil during the second period of life.

Then the impulse arises: The good that pleased you—this is what you must do! And what displeased you, you must not do. This principle of morality arises from what is already present in the human I, and a religious devotion toward the world arises in the spirit, which had been a thing of nature during the first period, and a thing of the soul during the second. The religious sense—and will applied to the religious impulse—becomes something that allows human beings to act as though God were acting in them. This becomes the expression of the I, not something imposed externally. Following puberty, if the child has developed in accordance with a true understanding of the human being, everything seems to arise as though born from human nature itself.

As I have already suggested, in order that this can happen, we must consider the whole human being during the earthly pilgrimage from birth to death. It's easy to say that one will begin education by employing the principle of simply observing the child. Today people observe the child externally and experimentally, and from what they perceive in the child they think they can discern the method of teaching. This is impossible, since, as we have seen, a teacher whose uncontrolled choleric temperament leads to angry behavior sows a seed that will remain hidden, and later develop as gout, rheumatism, and disease of the whole organism.

This is what happens in many other relationships; we must keep in mind the earthly life of the whole human being. We must remember this when we are concerned with an event in a particular life period. There are those who limit themselves to a triviality often known as "visual instruction." They entrench themselves behind the rule—as obvious as it is foolish—that children should be shown only what they can comprehend, and they fall into absurdities that could drive a person crazy. This principle must be replaced by that deeper principle that helps us to understand what it means for the vitality of a person when, at the age of forty, a sudden realization occurs: For the first time I can understand what that respected authority thought and accomplished earlier. I absorbed it because, to me, that individual embodied truth, goodness, and beauty. Now I have the opportunity to draw from the depths what I heard in those days.

When things are reinvigorated in this way, there is an infinitely rejuvenating and vitalizing effect on later life. The human being is deprived of all this at a later age if the teacher fails to insure that there actually is something in the depths that will be understood only later on. The world becomes empty and barren, unless something can arise anew again and again from the essence of human nature—something that permeates outer perception with soul and spirit. Therefore, when we educate this way, we give the human being full freedom and vitality for the rest of life.

Materialism and Spirit in Education

At this point, let me mention something I have often spoken of. A true teacher must always keep in view all of human life. A teacher must, for example, be able to see the wonderful element that is present in many older people, whose very presence brings a kind of blessing without much in the way of words; a kind of blessing is contained in every gesture. This is a characteristic of many people who stand at the threshold of death. From where does this come? Such individuals have this quality because, during childhood, they developed devotion naturally. Such reverence and devotion during childhood later becomes the capacity to bless. We may say that at the end of earthly life, people cannot stretch out their hands in blessing if they have not learned to fold them in prayer during childhood. The capacity for blessing when one grows old and comes near the threshold of death originates with folding one's hands in prayer with reverent, childhood devotion. Everything visible as a seed in the child will develop into good or evil fruit as the person progresses farther along in earthly life. And this is something else that must be continually within view in order to develop a genuine teaching method based on real life in education.

Thus—at least in rough outline—we have the foundation for an attempt to bring anthroposophy to fruit in education through Waldorf schools. This education conference should illuminate what has been attempted in this way and practiced for some years. It has been illuminated from various perspectives and we have shown what the students themselves have accomplished—though, in relation to this, much has yet to be demonstrated and discussed.

At the beginning of today's lecture, I was addressed with loving words from two sides, for which I am heartily grateful; after all, what could be done with impulses, however beautiful, if there were no one to realize them through devotion and self-sacrifice? Therefore, my gratitude goes to the Waldorf teachers who try to practice what needs to underlie this kind of renewal in education. My gratitude also goes out to today's youth, young men and women who, through their own educational experiences, understand the true aims of Waldorf education. One would be happy indeed if the cordiality felt by young people for Waldorf education carried their message to our civilization and culture.

I believe I am speaking for the hearts of all of you when I respond with words of gratitude to those who have spoken so lovingly, because, more than anything else, education needs human beings who will accomplish these goals. A painter or sculptor can work in solitude and say that even if people do not see the work, the gods do. When a teacher performs spiritual actions for earthly existence, however, the fulfillment of such activities can be expected only in communion with those who help to realize them in the physical realm of the senses.

As teachers and educators, this impulse must live in our awareness, especially in our time. Therefore, as we conclude these lectures—this lecture must be the last, since I am wanted elsewhere and cannot remain in Stuttgart—allow me to point to something. Based on anthroposophy and not forcing it on people as a worldview—based on anthroposophy because it gives a true knowledge of the human being in body, soul, and spirit—let me conclude by saying that this education serves, in the most practical way possible, the deepest needs and conditions of our modern civilization. The people of Central Europe can hope for a future only if their actions and thoughts arise from such impulses.

What is our most intense suffering? By trying to characterize our education I repeatedly had to point out that we stand with reverent awe before the human I-being placed in the world by divine powers helping to develop that I. The human I is not truly understood unless it is understood in spirit; it is denied when understood only in matter. It is primarily the I that has suffered because of our contemporary materialistic life, because of ignorance, because of the wrong concept of the human I.

This is primarily due to the fact that—while we have hammered away at perception of matter and at activity in matter—spirit has been shattered, and with it the I.

If we place limits on knowledge, as is common, saying that we cannot enter the realm of spirit, this implies only that we cannot enter the human realm. To limit knowledge means that we remove the human being from the world as far as knowing is concerned. How can a soul be educated if it has been eliminated by materialistic concepts? Elimination of the soul was characteristic of the kind of materialism we have just passed through, and it still prevails throughout human activity.

What has happened in the materialistic attitude of the more modern time? It is an attitude that, as I have said, was justified from a different perspective because it had to enter human evolution at some point, but now it must pass away. In expressing this attitude, we may say that the human being has surrendered the I to matter—connected it to matter. Consequently, however, the genuine, living method of teaching, the real life of education has been frozen; only external techniques can survive in a civilization bound by matter. But, matter oppresses people. Matter confines each person within the bodily nature, and each individual thus becomes more or less isolated in soul. Unless we find other human beings in spirit, we become isolated souls, since human beings cannot, in fact, be found in the body.

Thus, our civilization's materialistic view has produced an age when human beings pass each other by, because their perceptions are all connected with bodily nature. People cry out for a social life out of the intellect, and at the same time develop in their feelings an asocial indifference toward one another as well as a lack of mutual understanding. Souls who are isolated in individual bodies pass one another by, whereas souls who awaken the spirit within to find spirit itself also find themselves, as human beings, in communion with other human beings. Real community will blossom from the present chaos only when people find the spirit—when, living together in spirit, they find each other.

The great longing of today's youth is to discover the human being. The youth movement came from this cry. A few days ago when the young people here came together, it became evident that this cry has been transformed into a cry for spirit, through the realization that the human being can be found only when spirit is found; if spirit is lost, we lose one another.

Last evening, I tried to show how we can find knowledge of the world—how the human being living on earth in body, soul, and spirit can develop out of such knowledge. I tried to show how a worldview can develop into an experience of the cosmos, and the Sun and Moon may be seen in everything that grows and flourishes on Earth. When we educate young people with this kind of background, we will properly develop the experience of immortality, the divine, the eternally religious element in the growing child, and we implant in the child's being an immortal aspect destined for further progress, which we must carry in spirit through the gate of death.

This particular aspect of education is not what we are discussing here. The relationship between education and the human I, as well as culture, is what we had to look at first. Nevertheless, we may be sure of one thing; if people are educated properly on Earth, the heavenly being will also be educated properly, since the heavenly being lives within the earthly being. When we educate the earthly being correctly, we also promote the true development of the heavenly being through the tiny amount of progress that we make possible between birth and death.

In this way we come to terms with a view that progresses, in the true sense, to a universal knowledge—a knowledge that understands the need for human cooperation in the great spiritual cosmos, which is also revealed in the realm of the senses.

True education recognizes that human beings are coworkers in building humankind. This is what I meant yesterday when I described the view of life that I said must form the background of all teaching and education.

From this, it follows that we cannot understand the world as a one-sided subject of the head alone. It is untrue to say that we can understand the world through ideas and concepts. And it is equally false to say that the world can be understood through feeling alone. It has to be understood through ideas and feeling, as well as through the will; human beings will understand the world only when divine spirit descends into will. Humankind will also be understood then—not through one aspect, but through the whole being. We need a worldview not just for the intellect, but for the whole human being—for human thinking, feeling, and willing—a concept of the world that discovers the world in the human body, soul, and spirit.

Only those who rediscover the world in the human being, and who see the world in human beings, can have a true concept of the world; because, just as the visible world is reflected in the eye, the entire human being exists as an eye of spirit, soul, and body, reflecting the whole cosmos. Such a reflection cannot be perceived externally; it must be experienced from within. Then it is not just an appearance, like an ordinary mirrored image; it is an inner reality. Thus, in the process of education, the world becomes human, and the human being discovers the world in the self.

Working this way in education, we feel that the human race would be disrupted if all human experience were tied to matter, because, when they deny their own being, souls do not find one another but lose themselves. When we move to spirit, we find other human beings. Community, in the true sense of the word, must be established through spirit. Human beings must find themselves in spirit; then they can unite with others.

If worlds are to be created out of human actions, then the world must be seen in human beings.

In conclusion, allow me to express what was in the back of my mind while I was speaking to you. What I said here was intended as a consideration of education in the personal and cultural life of the present time. Now, in conclusion, let me put this in other words that include all I have wanted to say.

> To spend oneself in matter
> is to grind down souls.
>
> To find oneself in the spirit
> is to unite human beings.
>
> To see oneself in all humanity
> is to construct worlds.

Further Reading

Basic Works by Rudolf Steiner

Anthroposophical Leading Thoughts: Anthroposophy as a Path of Knowledge: The Michael Mystery, Rudolf Steiner Press, London, 1985.

Anthroposophy (A Fragment), Anthroposophic Press, Hudson, NY, 1996.

An Autobiography, Steinerbooks, Blauvelt, NY, 1977.

Christianity as Mystical Fact, Anthroposophic Press, Hudson, NY, 1997.

The Foundation Stone / The Life, Nature, and Cultivation of Anthroposophy, Rudolf Steiner Press, London, 1996.

How to Know Higher Worlds: A Modern Path of Initiation, Anthroposophic Press, Hudson, NY, 1994.

Intuitive Thinking as a Spiritual Path: A Philosophy of Freedom, Anthroposophic Press, Hudson, NY, 1995 (previously translated as *Philosophy of Spiritual Activity*).

An Outline of Esoteric Science, Anthroposophic Press, Hudson, NY, 1997 (previous translation titled *An Outline of Occult Science*).

A Road to Self-Knowledge and The Threshold of the Spiritual World, Rudolf Steiner Press, London, 1975.

Theosophy: An Introduction to the Spiritual Processes in Human Life and in the Cosmos, Anthroposophic Press, Hudson, NY, 1994.

Books by Other Authors

Anschütz, Marieke. *Children and Their Temperaments*, Floris Books, Edinburgh, 1995.

Barnes, Henry. *A Life for the Spirit: Rudolf Steiner in the Crosscurrents of Our Time*. Anthroposophic Press, Hudson, NY, 1997.

Britz-Crecelius, Heidi. *Children at Play: Using Waldorf Principles to Foster Childhood Development*, Park Street Press, Rochester, VT, 1996.

Budd, Christopher Houghton (ed). *Rudolf Steiner, Economist: Articles & Essays*, New Economy Publications, Canterbury, UK, 1996.

Carlgren, Frans. *Education Towards Freedom: Rudolf Steiner Education: A Survey of the Work of Waldorf Schools Throughout the World*, Lanthorn Press, East Grinstead, England, 1993.

Childs, Gilbert. *Education and Beyond: Steiner and the Problems of Modern Society*, Floris Books, Edinburgh, 1996.

—— *Understanding Your Temperament! A Guide to the Four Temperaments*, Sophia Books, London, 1995.

Childs, Dr. Gilbert and Sylvia Childs. *Your Reincarnating Child*, Sophia Books/Rudolf Steiner Press, London, 1995.

Edmunds, L. Francis. *Renewing Education: Selected Writings on Steiner Education*, Hawthorn Press, Stroud, UK, 1992.

——*Rudolf Steiner Education: The Waldorf School*, Rudolf Steiner Press, London, 1992.

Fenner, Pamela Johnson and Karen L. Rivers, eds. *Waldorf Student Reading List*, third edition, Michaelmas Press, Amesbury, MA, 1995.

Finser, Torin M. *School as a Journey: The Eight-Year Odyssey of a Waldorf Teacher and His Class*, Anthroposophic Press, Hudson, NY, 1994.

Gabert, Erich. *Educating the Adolescent: Discipline or Freedom*, Anthroposophic Press, Hudson, NY, 1988.

Gardner, John Fentress. *Education in Search of the Spirit: Essays on American Education,* Anthroposophic Press, Hudson, NY, 1996.

——*Youth Longs to Know: Explorations of the Spirit in Education,* Anthroposophic Press, Hudson, NY, 1997.

Gatto, John Taylor. *Dumbing Us Down: The Hidden Curriculum of Compulsory Schooling,* New Society, Philadelphia, 1992.

Harwood, A. C. *The Recovery of Man in Childhood: A Study in the Educational Work of Rudolf Steiner,* The Myrin Institute of New York, New York, 1992.

Heider, Molly von. *Looking Forward: Games, rhymes and exercises to help children develop their learning abilities,* Hawthorn Press, Stroud, UK, 1995.

Heydebrand, Caroline von, *Childhood: A Study of the Growing Child,* Anthroposophic Press, Hudson, NY, 1995.

Jaffke, Freya. *Work and Play in Early Childhood,* Anthroposophic Press, Hudson, NY, 1996.

Large, Martin. *Who's Bringing Them Up? How to Break the T.V. Habit!* Hawthorn Press, Stroud, UK, 1990.

Logan, Arnold, ed. *A Garden of Songs for Singing and Piping at Home and School,* Windrose Publishing and Educational Services, Chatham, NY, 1996.

McDermott, Robert. *The Essential Steiner: Basic Writings of Rudolf Steiner.* HarperCollins, New York, 1984.

Maher, Stanford and Yvonne Bleach. *"Putting the Heart Back into Teaching": A Manual for Junior Primary Teachers,* Novalis Press, Cape Town, South Africa, 1996.

Maher, Stanford and Ralph Shepherd. *Standing on the Brink—An Education for the 21st Century: Essays on Waldorf Education,* Novalis Press, Cape Town, South Africa, 1995.

Nobel, Agnes. *Educating through Art: The Steiner School Approach,* Floris Books, Edinburgh, 1996.

Pusch, Ruth, ed. *Waldorf Schools Volume I: Kindergarten and Early Grades*, Mercury Press, Spring Valley, NY, 1993.

—— *Waldorf Schools Volume II: Upper Grades and High School*, Mercury Press, Spring Valley, NY, 1993.

Richards, M. C. *Opening Our Moral Eye*, Lindisfarne Books, Hudson, NY, 1996.

Spock, Marjorie. *Teaching as a Lively Art*, Anthroposophic Press, Hudson, NY, 1985.

THE FOUNDATIONS
OF WALDORF EDUCATION

THE FIRST FREE WALDORF SCHOOL opened its doors in Stuttgart, Germany, in September, 1919, under the auspices of Emil Molt, the Director of the Waldorf Astoria Cigarette Company and a student of Rudolf Steiner's spiritual science and particularly of Steiner's call for social renewal.

It was only the previous year—amid the social chaos following the end of World War I—that Emil Molt, responding to Steiner's prognosis that truly human change would not be possible unless a sufficient number of people received an education that developed the whole human being, decided to create a school for his workers' children. Conversations with the minister of education and with Rudolf Steiner, in early 1919, then led rapidly to the forming of the first school.

Since that time, more than six hundred schools have opened around the globe—from Italy, France, Portugal, Spain, Holland, Belgium, Great Britain, Norway, Finland, and Sweden to Russia, Georgia, Poland, Hungary, Romania, Israel, South Africa, Australia, Brazil, Chile, Peru, Argentina, Japan, and others—making the Waldorf school movement the largest independent school movement in the world. The United States, Canada, and Mexico alone now have more than 120 schools.

Although each Waldorf school is independent, and although there is a healthy oral tradition going back to the first Waldorf teachers and to Steiner himself, as well as a growing body of secondary literature, the true foundations of the Waldorf method and spirit remain the many lectures that Rudolf Steiner gave on the subject. For five years (1919–24), Rudolf Steiner, while simultaneously working on many other fronts, tirelessly dedicated himself to the dissemination of the idea of Waldorf education. He gave manifold lectures to teachers, parents, the general public, and even the children themselves. New schools were founded. The movement grew.

While many of Steiner's foundational lectures have been translated and published in the past, some have never appeared in English, and many have been virtually unobtainable for years. To remedy this situation and to establish a coherent basis for Waldorf education, Anthroposophic Press has decided to publish the complete series of Steiner lectures and writings on education in a uniform series. This series will thus constitute an authoritative foundation for work in educational renewal, for Waldorf teachers, parents, and educators generally.

RUDOLF STEINER'S LECTURES
(AND WRITINGS) ON EDUCATION

I. *Allgemeine Menschenkunde als Grundlage der Pädagogik. Pädagogischer Grundkurs,* 14 Lectures, Stuttgart, 1919 (GA 293). Previously *Study of Man. The Foundations of Human Experience* (Anthroposophic Press, 1996).

II. *Erziehungskunst Methodische-Didaktisches,* 14 Lectures, Stuttgart, 1919 (GA 294). *Practical Advice to Teachers* (Rudolf Steiner Press, 1988).

III. *Erziehungskunst,* 15 Discussions, Stuttgart, 1919 (GA 295). *Discussions with Teachers* (Anthroposophic Press, 1997).

IV. *Die Erziehungsfrage als soziale Frage,* 6 Lectures, Dornach, 1919 (GA 296). *Education as a Force for Social Change* (previously *Education as a Social Problem*) (Anthroposophic Press, 1997).

V. *Die Waldorf Schule und ihr Geist,* 6 Lectures, Stuttgart and Basel, 1919 (GA 297). *The Spirit of the Waldorf School* (Anthroposophic Press, 1995).

VI. *Rudolf Steiner in der Waldorfschule, Vorträge und Ansprachen,* Stuttgart, 1919–1924 (GA 298). *Rudolf Steiner in the Waldorf School: Lectures and Conversations* (Anthroposophic Press, 1996).

VII. *Geisteswissenschaftliche Sprachbetrachtungen,* 6 Lectures, Stuttgart, 1919 (GA 299). *The Genius of Language* (Anthroposophic Press, 1995).

VIII. *Konferenzen mit den Lehren der Freien Waldorfschule 1919–1924,* 3 Volumes (GA 300). *Conferences with Teachers* (Steiner Schools Fellowship, 1986, 1987, 1988, 1989).

IX. *Die Erneuerung der Pädagogisch-didaktischen Kunst durch Geisteswissenschaft,* 14 Lectures, Basel, 1920 (GA 301). *The Renewal of Education* (Kolisko Archive Publications for Steiner Schools Fellowship Publications, Michael Hall, Forest Row, East Sussex, UK, 1981).

X. *Menschenerkenntnis und Unterrichtsgestaltung,* 8 Lectures, Stuttgart, 1921 (GA 302). Previously *The Supplementary Course—Upper School* and *Waldorf Education for Adolescence. Education for Adolescents* (Anthroposophic Press, 1996).

XI. *Erziehung und Unterricht aus Menschenerkenntnis,* 9 Lectures, Stuttgart, 1920, 1922, 1923 (GA 302a). The first four lectures available as *Balance in Teaching* (Mercury Press, 1982); last three lectures as *Deeper Insights into Education* (Anthroposophic Press, 1988).

XII. *Die Gesunder Entwicklung des Menschenwesens,* 16 Lectures, Dornach, 1921–22 (GA 303). *Soul Economy and Waldorf Education* (Anthroposophic Press, 1986).

XIII. *Erziehungs- und Unterrichtsmethoden auf Anthroposophischer Grundlage,* 9 Public Lectures, various cities, 1921–22 (GA 304). *Waldorf Education and Anthroposophy 1* (Anthroposophic Press, 1995).

XIV. *Anthroposophische Menschenkunde und Pädagogik,* 9 Public Lectures, various cities, 1923–24 (GA 304a). *Waldorf Education and Anthroposophy 2* (Anthroposophic Press, 1996).

XV. *Die geistig-seelischen Grundkräfte der Erziehungskunst,* 12 Lectures, 1 Special Lecture, Oxford 1922 (GA 305). *The Spiritual Ground of Education* (Garber Publications, 1989).

XVI. *Die pädagogisch Praxis vom Gesichtspunkte geisteswissenschaftlicher Menschenerkenntnis,* 8 Lectures, Dornach, 1923 (GA 306). *The Child's Changing Consciousness As the Basis of Pedagogical Practice* (Anthroposophic Press, 1996).

XVII. *Gegenwärtiges Geistesleben und Erziehung,* 4 Lectures, Ilkeley, 1923 (GA 307). *A Modern Art of Education* (Rudolf Steiner Press, 1981) and *Education and Modern Spiritual Life* (Garber Publications, n.d.).

XVIII. *Die Methodik des Lehrens und die Lebensbedingungen des Erziehens,* 5 Lectures, Stuttgart, 1924 (GA 308). *The Essentials of Education* (Anthroposophic Press, 1997).

XIX. *Anthroposophische Pädagogik und ihre Voraussetzungen,* 5 Lectures, Bern, 1924 (GA 309). *The Roots of Education* (Anthroposophic Press, 1997).

XX. *Der pädagogische Wert der Menschenerkenntnis und der Kulturwert der Pädagogik,* 10 Public Lectures, Arnheim, 1924 (GA 310). *Human Values in Education* (Rudolf Steiner Press, 1971).

XXI. *Die Kunst des Erziehens aus dem Erfassen der Menschenwesenheit,* 7 Lectures, Torquay, 1924 (GA 311). *The Kingdom of Childhood* (Anthroposophic Press, 1995).

XXII. *Geisteswissenschaftliche Impulse zur Entwicklung der Physik. Erster naturwissenschaftliche Kurs: Licht, Farbe, Ton—Masse, Elektrizität, Magnetismus,* 10 Lectures, Stuttgart, 1919–20 (GA 320). *The Light Course* (Steiner Schools Fellowship,1977).

XXIII. *Geisteswissenschaftliche Impulse zur Entwicklung der Physik. Zweiter naturwissenschaftliche Kurs: die Wärme auf der Grenze positiver und negativer Materialität,* 14 Lectures, Stuttgart, 1920 (GA 321). *The Warmth Course* (Mercury Press, 1988).

XXIV. *Das Verhältnis der verschiedenen naturwissenschaftlichen Gebiete zur Astronomie. Dritter naturwissenschaftliche Kurs: Himmelskunde in Beziehung zum Menschen und zur Menschenkunde,* 18 Lectures, Stuttgart, 1921 (GA 323). Available in typescript only as "The Relation of the Diverse Branches of Natural Science to Astronomy."

XXV. *The Education of the Child and Early Lectures on Education* (A collection) (Anthroposophic Press, 1996).

XXVI. Miscellaneous.

Index

abdominal system, 63. *See also*
    illness
abstract ideas, danger of, 51-52,
    67, 70
aging, 76-77
anatomy, 37-38
angels, 62-63
anger, 9
animals, teaching about, 62-65.
    See also Goethe, Wolfgang
    von
anthroposophy, 3, 17, 55-56,
    68, 77-78. *See also*
    Waldorf education
art, 72-73
    in second stage, 28-34, 69-70
arthritis, 9. *See also* illness
assertiveness, 33-34
asthma, 33
astral body, 48, 64, 66
    and music, 46-47, 51, 62, 66.
    See also etheric body; physical
    body
astronomy, 55

birth, 20
block teaching, 53.
    See also Waldorf education
Bohemian-Magyar
    brotherhoods, 38

breathing process, 23, 33, 42-
    43. *See also* illness
bull, 62-63. *See also* animals

childhood. *See* first stage of
    childhood; second stage of
    childhood; third stage of
    childhood
choleric temperament, 7-9, 75-
    76. *See also* temperament
circulatory system, 23, 29, 42-
    43. *See also* illness
college, 15
contraction, cosmic principle
    of, 19, 55-56, 57. *See also*
    Goethe, Johann Wolfgang
    von

Dark Ages. *See* Middle Ages
depression, 10. *See also* illness
development, 5-6
digestive system, 9, 23, 28, 33-
    34, 42-43, 54-55, 63. *See
    also* illness
doctor. *See* illness, medicine

eagle, 62-63. *See also* animals
Earth, 54-60
East, education in, 14
Easter, 58, 60

and nineteenth century, 10-11, 73
See also phlegmatic temperament; Middle Ages; modern worldview; nineteenth century
medicine, 9, 28. *See also* illness
melancholic temperament, 11-12. *See also* temperament; illness
metabolic system, 9, 62-63. *See also* illness
meteorology, 59
Middle Ages, 17-18, 25-26, 36-38. *See also* materialism; modern worldview; nineteenth century
mineral kingdom, 1
modern worldview, 12-13, 25-26. *See also* materialism
monastic schools, 18
Moon, 56-60
moral realm, 72, 73, 75
movements, and education, 41-42. *See also* second stage of childhood
music, 44-45
  and astral body, 62, 65-66
  See also astral body; second stage of childhood

natural science, 1-2, 20, 36
  and anthroposophy, 39-40
nervous disease, 10-11, 47. *See also* illness
nineteenth century, 10-11, 36-37, 73. *See also* materialism; modern worldview; Middle Ages
nutrition, 59

Oken, Lorenz, 63

pathologies, cultural, 10
philology, 47-48
phlegmatic temperament, 10-11. *See also* illness; temperament
physical body, 2, 28, 45, 51, 60, 64, 66, 78. *See also* astral body; etheric body; natural science
physiology, 17, 35-36, 46-48
pictographic writing, 32
pictures, in education, 32-33, 60-62, 65-66. *See also* first stage of life, second stage of life; Goethe, Johann Wolfgang von; plants
plants, 55-61, 73-74. *See also* Goethe, Johann Wolfgang von
pleasure, as morality, 71
pre-earthly life. *See* reincarnation
priestly attitude, of the teacher, 23-25, 31, 69. *See also* first stage of childhood; religious attitude
proof, what constitutes, 17-20
psychology, 2, 17, 28
puberty, 42, 69
  and astral body, 65-67
  and intellect, 72-73 morality, 75
  See also third stage of childhood

reading, 35, 51-54. *See also* language; writing
rebirth. *See* reincarnation

DURING THE LAST TWO DECADES of the nineteenth century the Austrian-born Rudolf Steiner (1861–1925) became a respected and well-published scientific, literary, and philosophical scholar, particularly known for his work on Goethe's scientific writings. After the turn of the century he began to develop his earlier philosophical principles into an approach to methodical research of psychological and spiritual phenomena.

His multifaceted genius has led to innovative and holistic approaches in medicine, philosophy, religion, education (Waldorf schools), special education, economics, agriculture (Biodynamic method), science, architecture, drama, the new arts of speech and eurythmy, and other fields of activity. In 1924 he founded the General Anthroposophical Society, which today has branches throughout the world.

· · · · · · · · · · ·

For an informative catalog of the work of Rudolf Steiner
and other anthroposophical authors please contact

ANTHROPOSOPHIC PRESS
3390 Route 9, Hudson, NY 12534
TEL: 518-851-2054
FAX: 518-851-2047